"*Blind But Now I See* gives evidence of modern-day miracles occurring through donor tissue and organ transplantation. Corneal transplants in both eyes restored Brenda's sight as well as her quality of life. I too, have benefited from a major organ transplant. I was given seven days to live and on the seventh day received a life-giving and life-changing liver transplant. The spiritual principles in this book will help anyone take up their bed and live life to its fullest."

*Erskine Gillespie*
*Organ Transplant Recipient*

"I am very proud of Brenda and how she has taken the struggle with her eyes and symbolized it as one of God's purposes for her life. She has given readers concise and practical advice on how to face any challenge and demonstrates to us what it really means to look at life through our spiritual eyes. The basic spiritual principles outlined in her book are simple but in no way are they easy. This author puts into focus those disciplines necessary to help us face and overcome the stresses and uncertainties that life places before us."

*Elder Barbara Miller*
*Lithonia, Georgia*

"This book should not be read like a novel. Take time to absorb its message on coming out of whatever holds you in bondage. Learning how to live with a devastating diagnosis or circumstance without giving up is a remarkable testimony for anyone. I'm practicing the suggestions, drawing closer to God, and learning to view life more spiritually."

*Reginald Edward Nichols*
*Knoxville, Tennessee*

"Mrs. Nichols expertly blends her testimony of challenged vision with indelible life principles which offers hope and encouragement to any diagnosis or life challenge. Readers will benefit immensely from the enlightening of their eyes and minds to see the truth in any matter, thus evolving as a better person because of the experience."

*Rev. Earnestine Hunt*
*MBA Divinity, Chaplain, Memphis, Tennessee*

"We should not take our eyesight for granted. This is a good book to understand how a loved one experiences life living with impaired vision. My baby sister has put it out here for us to taste and see life through her KC eyes. A very good and inspirational read."

*Lillie Plunkett,*
*Case Management, Memphis, Tennessee*

"While in the Intensive Care Waiting Room, God had me reveal to this author without prior knowledge of her testimony that her book will give sight and insight to the blind both natural and spiritual. It will open blinded eyes. People will look at things in a different aspect and proclaim, *I can see clearly now!* This is a testament of God's creation *'in the beginning'* handy work."

*Prophetess Darnish Proctor,*
*Chaplain-Prison Ministry, Memphis, Tennessee*

# Blind

## But Now I See

Brenda Joyce Nichols

# Blind

## But Now I See

Living with Keratoconus

Foreword by Dr. Scott McGregor

TATE PUBLISHING & *Enterprises*

Published by Tate Publishing & Enterprises, LLC
127 E. Trade Center Terrace | Mustang, Oklahoma 73064 USA
1.888.361.9473 | www.tatepublishing.com

Tate Publishing is committed to excellence in the publishing industry. The company reflects the philosophy established by the founders, based on Psalm 68:11,
*"The Lord gave the word and great was the company of those who published it."*

Book design copyright © 2008 by Tate Publishing, LLC. All rights reserved.
*Cover design by Nathan Harmony*
*Interior design by Tyler Evans*

Published in the United States of America

ISBN: 978-1-60604-825-2
1. Biography & Autobiography : Medical
2. Religion : Christian Life : Inspirational
08.12.08

I dedicate this book to everyone who has been liberated from anything that held them in bondage and darkness.

*"Depression loses its power when fresh vision pierces the darkness."*
*—Peter Sinclair—*[1]

# Acknowledgements

I have attempted to write this book several times within the last two years. Each time, its purpose was more intent and filled with an utmost urgency.

I thank God for this writing mandate and requiring my best work. I've done what he has told me based on scriptural instructions. "That I may publish with the voice of thanksgiving and tell of all thou wondrous works" (Psalms 26:7).

Lovingly, to my husband, Reginold, who is the wind beneath my wings, and our children, Roslyn, Reggie, and Ryan; each of you has endured this journey with me from an up-close-and-personal view. Thanks for hanging in here with me at all times. And to EJ, our first grandchild, who brings an added measure of joy to our quiver, I joyously exclaim, "I see you!"

I extend thanks to my prayer partners, Minister Jackie Alexander and Reverend Earnestine Hunt, and my loving niece, Joyce Prewitt McMillan, for their steadfast assistance in echoing God's requirements to publish and tell my story.

A special thanks to Pastor Monte Campbell for the outpouring of God's "Rhema Word" into my life. Thank you,

New Destiny Church family, Barbara Bailey Burks, Toi Wilkins Harris, Denise Jackson, and Barbara Spencer for your witness assignments. Indeed, our church family is a chosen people that God has joined together.

A heartfelt hug of love and appreciation to my family, extended family, prayer partners, coworkers, and friends, who have cried, laughed, held my hand, and walked through these experiences with me. Absolutely, I could not have endured this course alone.

An extra big hug to Jason Hunt (KC eye drawings), Phyllis Hazley and Michelle Brown. Each of you came to my rescue with last minute assistance.

I extend my gracious appreciation to those I've met along the way as I've enlarged my territory: Lee Williams and the Mid-South Eye Bank, Kip Alexander and the Mid-South Transplant Foundation, Marcus McDaniel and Adams Corporation, Catherine Warren and the National Keratoconus Foundation, Discovery Eye Foundation, Rusty Kelly and the Eye Bank Association of America, Paul Hopkins and the River City Awareness Group, Elio Spinello, and Ian McCain. I also extend thanks to the NKCF message board members who have shared their KC stories with me to publish to the world with a voice of thanksgiving.

Lastly, to the Tate Publishing team of professionals. There is no doubt in my mind that our paths connected to carry out God's great commission of publishing. A special thanks to Donna Chumley, April Larsen, Nathan Harmony, Tyler Evans, Josh Kilbourne, and the Marketing department for your professional expertise and guidance.

It is with honor that I now "commit my work unto the Lord and my plans will succeed" (Proverbs 16:3).

# Table of Contents

# Foreword

While I have had the pleasure to work for more years than I wish to admit caring for keratoconus patients, this is the first time I have read such a complete account of the effect the disease can have on a person.

As a doctor and daily advisor on the National Keratoconus Foundation's Web site, I read every day the problems faced by patients. My job as a medical advisor on the foundation's Web site is to advise these often-terrified people. It saddens me that each person must go through their own denial, grief, acceptance, and, finally, action phases. However, there is no road map to guide them.

Mrs. Nichols has encapsulated the whole experience from the first day of diagnosis through all the trials that led to bilateral transplants. I found her book fascinating even as a doctor specializing in keratoconus, as it gave me an insight into the life and struggles of these patients. The most wonderful feature is that she offers her own form of advice and council. Her belief in God and his purpose for us all has guided her journey through this disease.

When Mrs. Nichols came to the Contact Lens Institute

in Dallas, Texas, she was wearing eyeglasses. I knew her case would be challenging, but I did not realize how bad her problem was. Her vision had been rated using special low vision charts and had found her to have Feinbloom 10/20. This is equal to the 20/40–20/50 range in normal Snellen vision charts usually used in doctors' offices. She also had been given two low vision devices to allow her to perform daily tasks. Her eyeglass prescription had 8.50 units of astigmatism in the left and 10.00 units in the right. Anything over the level of 2.00 units is considered severe and impossible to fit with routine contact lenses. Mrs. Nichols had five times that amount.

I was able to fit her with the Mac-G Lenses, for which I have been issued a full patent from the United States Patent and Trademark Office. In two quick fitting sets of Mac-G Lenses, she was able to see at the 20/15–20/20 range. She reports that the comfort level of the Mac-G Lenses allows her extremely long hours of wear and excellent vision. The fitting of this unique gas permeable lens brings unprecedented success for the twenty-first century practitioner.

As I have told my patients for years, nearly thirty million Americans get up every day and put on a pair of contact lenses. The reason is unimportant. The labels are unimportant. All that matters is that vision can be restored and people can lead normal and functional lives. Mrs. Nichols has lived just such a life. She didn't shrink away into disability; she took her disease head-on and conquered it. It is unfortunate that modern science let her down on many occasions and left her to seek answers on her own, and that is why this book should be read by every patient with keratoconus and every family member. She offers guidance to keratoconus patients and families.

Additionally, there is so much misinformation out there

that it is easy for a new patient to be terrified by a fear of blindness. However, Mrs. Nichols has seen fit to include a lengthy section of testimonials from other keratoconus patients to illustrate their plights. I personally know many of these people via my association with the National Keratoconus Foundation, and their stories are real and true.

On a personal note, ten years ago, I was partially paralyzed in a terrible automobile accident, and it took twenty-one open spinal surgeries to repair all the damage. But God allowed me to recover. I remember thinking that death would be so much easier, and why did God see fit to keep me alive? Every day in my office patients and their families burst into tears of joy as the specialty lenses I use restores their vision. It is in that moment that I smile inside, and I know why God spared me. These are my patients, but they are all his children; and we all know any parent will do anything for their children. So, God sent me back to the exam room, where every patient could walk out of my office exclaiming, "I once was blind, but now I see."

I strongly recommend this book to anyone facing keratoconus or has a loved one affected by this disease. Keratoconus is not a blinding disease when properly treated. There is help, and there is hope.

*Dr. Scott McGregor, O. D.*
*Contact Lens Institute of Dallas*
*Member–Medical Advisory Board*
*National Keratoconus Foundation*
*Web site: www.drscottmcgregor.com*

# Introduction

I believe that everybody has a story. In between birth and death, the pages of our stories are being written. In this book, I will share with you a mere fraction of my life's story. You will learn about an eye disease known as Keratoconus, commonly referred to as KC that labeled me as being functionally blind. The only option to correct my vision was to wear specialty contact lenses, and when contact lenses could no longer help me, the other alternative was to have corneal transplants.

Just as I believe that everyone has a story, I also believe that most people, if not everyone, can identify with having a "thorn in the flesh." A thorn can be something in your life that will not go away. Don't make the mistake of assuming that every trial or nuisance in your life can be called a thorn in the flesh. A thorn is about a situation that is locking in and it's not likely to change anytime soon.

I believe that God gives us thorns for our benefit. KC is my thorn. I didn't want this book to be just about my thorn in the flesh, but I want every reader to see your thorn as that one thing that is shaping and perfecting your life according to God's purpose for you.

God purposed me with KC for a reason. Psalms 139:13–16, which paraphrased states, I am fearfully and wonderfully made and that God knitted me together in my mother's womb. His eyes saw my unformed body. All the days ordained to me were written in God's book before one of them ever came to be. Now, doesn't that show that God has plans for our lives? I'm so glad that he didn't consult me when he created me. Aren't you glad that he didn't consult you about you? Aren't you happy that God designed the master plan for your life?

The title of the book, *Blind But Now I See*, speaks volumes and brings liberation to whatever limitations that you may face. No matter what you may be going through, once you allow your mind to open fully and accept truth—darkness has to flee. It is then that we are set free spiritually, mentally, emotionally, and physically to accelerate to a higher level.

Each chapter is written in a way that allows you to give thought to your own situation as I share my testimony. Pay special attention to the quotes at the beginning of each chapter. Go inside yourself and meditate on each one. Ask the Holy Spirit to illuminate a special message or interpretation just for you.

It is my prayer that every person who reads this book will embrace their illness or circumstance as a God-given gift that enables you to draw closer to him. I pray that every eye that reads this book knows there is no problem, circumstance, or situation greater than God. I pray this book inspires you to see with 20/20 spiritual vision your own testimony and empowers you to tell others that God has purpose for your life and journey on this earth. I pray that these words will be received into the hearts of every eye that sees them and every mouth that confesses God willingly.

In addition, you will read testimonies from other KCers around the world, signifying that many of us are walking similar vision-challenged journeys. We are connected all over the world through sharing our diagnosis, lifting our prayers to the Lord, and encouraging one another along the way. Each story gives detailed evidence of how challenging it is to see, function, and live with KC on a daily basis. Take the time to read each one, and you will learn how things look through KC eyes. You will leave with a deeper appreciation for your gift of sharp, clear, and focused vision.

Now that I've taken the muzzle off my mouth and blinders off my eyes, I see the big picture. It is as though the Holy Spirit has given me 20/20 vision and I can see clearly why my testimony had to be put in a book and published to the world. Why? It is because God, our Heavenly Father, and our Lord and Savior, Jesus Christ, must be glorified through our testimonies.

God has brought so many of us through too many things for them to remain in journals and mentioned only in casual conversation. Psalms 26:7 states clearly, publish with the voice of thanksgiving and tell of all thou wondrous works. Therefore, I am convicted to open my mouth and broadcast his works. Ask yourself, "Am I here in living color as evidence that God is still in the miracle-working, deliverance, healing, and blessing business?" If your answer is *yes*, then you are commissioned as well to tell of all his wondrous works.

Go ahead and get your eye spectacles, magnifying glass, eye drops, or whatever is needed to help you see. Count your blessings if you don't need to gear up to see, because you're truly blessed. Most importantly, don't forget to put on your spiritual eyes. You'll need them to get the full panoramic version of the message that God wants you to receive.

To God be the glory!

# My Eye Story

"There are two great days in a person's life;
the day we are born and the day we discover why."
–William Barclay–[2]

Remember the adage "Be careful what you ask for because you just might get it"? It's safe to say that it happened to me. There was a time that I desperately wanted to wear eyeglasses. Simply because I thought they made you look smart and sophisticated. One day my wish came true.

In 1984, at the age of twenty-eight, I was officially diagnosed with keratoconus, KC for short. KC is an eye disease that can render its victims functionally blind. This eye disease has afforded me an opportunity to wear eyeglasses, rigid gas permeable contact lenses, hybrid soft contact lenses, eyeglasses and contact lenses together, two corneal transplants, more eyeglasses, and even more specialty contact lenses for the rest of my life.

Indeed, I say be careful what you wish or ask for because it just might come your way. Here's my story!

. . . . .

## *The Day God Showed Up!*

A good place to begin my eye story is the day that I learned just how much God loves me!

God sent his deliverance from my functional blindness on a warm, sunny Mother's Day Sunday morning in May of 1991. I had been living with my distorted KC vision for seven years. I was at my wit's end and had been on the cornea donor's transplant list for nine months.

My family was getting ready for church, and I was attempting to comb my daughter's hair. Parting her long thick hair was just too challenging for my blurred vision. Frustrated, I looked in the mirror to see how I was looking and could barely see my own blurred image clearly. With tears streaming down my face, I quietly hurried upstairs and closed the bedroom door. I had to cry out unto the Lord. He needed to come and see about me, and it needed to be quickly.

"Lord, if I must accept this fate, please don't leave me by myself," was my plea.

My husband came up and comforted me. Lovingly, his assurance to be with me whether I could see or not see was comforting. Unsuccessfully, I tried to convince him to take the children and go on to church without me. I really wanted to be alone so that I could have myself a pity party. After a few hours of feeling sorry for myself, I went downstairs to check on my family. My husband, nine-year-old daughter, six and four year old boys seemed happy and carefree, but I could see the concern on their faces.

Suddenly, my husband announced that everybody should get dressed because we were going out for a special Mother's Day brunch. As we were leaving the house, the telephone rang, and our daughter ran back to answer the ringing telephone.

"Mommy, it's your doctor!" she screamed loudly.

Indeed, it was Dr. Wood. "Angel, I have some eyes, and they're being flown into Memphis just for you," he exclaimed.

I was speechless. During the entire conversation, he kept calling me "Angel."

I could hear the inner voice deep within me quietly saying, *Yes, I love you, and I will never leave you alone.*

Dr. Wood wanted us to meet him at the hospital later that evening to perform the surgery. This was just too soon. I needed to make arrangements for my children. My job was having a staff conference the next day at a local conference center, and I had made all the arrangements and management needed me. This wasn't going the way I thought it would happen at all.

Can you believe after waiting nine months, I was saying it was happening to soon? Well, Dr. Wood scheduled me for surgery the following afternoon. He explained that he could keep the donated cornea on ice for only so long. Another young lady was coming from somewhere in Mississippi to receive the left cornea. He would do her surgery first and save me for last.

We were all overjoyed. We couldn't believe what had just happened. God showed up when I needed him the most. Just that quickly my sorrow was turned into joy. Most of my immediate family members were at their various churches for morning worship, and I had to wait until later that evening to announce the good news.

Can you see why this day ranks high in my testimony? There is no denying that God showed his love for me on that special Mother's Day. Oh, my soul blesses him continuously, and I dare not forget all his benefits unto me. "Bless the Lord, O my soul, and forget not all his benefits" (Psalms 103:2).

· · · · ·

## The Early Years

My dysfunctional eye journey started around the age of five. I have to mention that I am the youngest child of eight siblings, and they spoiled me sufficiently. Every morning, I would yell out to anyone who would come to my aide, "I'm up! Bring me a towel." Then one of my parents or siblings would appear with a hot face towel to place upon my stuck-together, crusty, mucus-filled eyelids.

Lovingly and gently, they would wipe my eyes until they were unstuck. I considered this a special bonding time with whomever came to see about me. As time went on, the face towels were thrown to me from the hallway, or I had to feel my way to the bathroom to get my own hot towel. *What happened to my special bonding time? Where did all the love go?*

My mother attributed my eye issues to hay fever and sinus drainage. She started a daily ritual of greasing me up with Vaseline, Vicks Vapor Rub, and handing me a roll of toilet tissue. Thereafter, I acquired my signature label of being the cute, pudgy, eye-rubbing, runny-eyed, snotty-nosed, toilet tissue-toting baby girl.

Looking back on those early years, I can see where KC may have presented its early signs. Keratoconus has been associated with atopic diseases, which include asthma, allergies, and eczema. A number of studies suggest that vigorous eye rubbing may contribute to the progression of keratoconus, and that persons should be discouraged from extreme eye rubbing. I was an eye-rubbing addict and received constant admonishment of this act from loved ones.

"Baby girl, if you don't stop rubbing your eyes, your eyeballs are going to fall out."

However, I was not under a doctor's care for allergy treatment, and I showed no signs of challenged vision. In school, I was a good scholar and great reader. It was natural for me to sit in the front of the classroom because it was where I could see the best. There was no reason to think that I had any eye disease. However, in the back of my mind, I had a gut feeling that I should've been wearing eyeglasses.

Through the years, I learned to cope with my sinus-draining issues with over-the-counter medicines. As a teenager, I learned the magic of eye makeup concealer to cover the dark circles around my eyes from extended eye burning and rubbing. Stylish sunglasses and reading glasses became my two best companions.

* * * * *

## The Diagnosis

In 1982, at age twenty-six, I had my first real eye exam, and I received my first pair of prescription eyeglasses. Since I had wanted to wear eyeglasses for so many years, why didn't I just go see an optometrist? As a working adult, health insurance was not an issue because I had coverage. In retrospect and seeing this thing with 20/20 spiritual vision, I'm convinced that my fate with eye doctors and KC was on a divine time line.

About three months after receiving my first pair of prescription eyeglasses, things went back to being out of focus. I recall seeing as though looking through a window on a rainy day. I was constantly wiping my eyeglasses, thinking that the lenses were smudgy, while daily asking myself, "Why is my vision so fuzzy wuzzy?"

In a span of eighteen months, I had gone through four pairs of eyeglasses. What was wrong with my optometrist? Why couldn't he write me a prescription that would last longer? Even more so, what was wrong with the company making my eyeglasses? This eye doctor had exceeded any normal margin of tolerance along with the "denial to pay" from my health insurance company. The optometrist was pocketing a loss, and so was I with out-of-pocket expenses. Enough was enough. I was going to have to find me another eye doctor.

On the day the optometrist referred me to an ophthalmologist, I had no idea that I was about to begin a significant journey to the discovery of one of my life's *whys*.

"Mrs. Nichols, you have an eye disease that is causing your sight to deteriorate rapidly. Your corneas are no longer round like a baseball but spiral like a football and bulging outward."

I felt like I was in a fog when the ophthalmologist was discussing the results of my eye tests. He continued to speak.

"At the rate the disease is progressing, eyeglasses act only as a Band-Aid. You will have to wear hard contact lenses sitting directly upon your corneas. I'm also pretty sure that when you get up in age, you will need corneal transplants in both of your eyes."

I can remember that day as if it were yesterday. You can imagine my surprise when I found out that the culprit were my corneas and not the eyeglasses. The only thing that kept me from losing my grip was when he said my eye disease was treatable and that I would probably be up in age when it came to corneal transplants.

I went home in a daze. Surely, God didn't give me my life to take away my eyesight. I was still my husband's bride after four years of marriage, mother to a beautiful eighteen-month-old baby girl, and had a promising career ahead of me. I was certain that "up in age" meant when I was in my seventies or eighties. I had plenty of time. I was still very young. Plus, God was not going to take away my sight; that just wasn't his plan for my life!

"For I know the plans I have for you, declares the Lord, plans to prosper you and not to harm you, plans to give you hope and a future" (Jeremiah 29:11).

· · · · ·

## Keratoconus (KC): Definition

First, it's important to know what the cornea is and its function. To locate the cornea, look at your eye in the mirror and you will see a clear surface covering the iris (the colored part of the eye) and pupil. This transparent tissue is the cornea. The cornea shields the inside of the eye from germs, dust, and other harmful matter. It shares this protective task with the sclera (the white of the eye). The cornea provides a barrier to protect the eye and focuses light on to the retina. The cornea is essential to good vision.

Keratoconus (kehr-uh-toh-koh-nus) is a disease of the cornea, the transparent curved windshield of the eye. The word "keratoconus" is formed by the joining of two Greek words: *kerato,* meaning cornea, and *konos,* meaning cone. Keratoconus, or *conical cornea,* means that the natural curvature of the normal cornea has changed to a cone-like bulge due to a thinning of the cornea. Scarring of the cornea often occurs. This affects vision, which may be blurred or distorted or may produce a ripple effect. As the disease progresses, the affected eyes become increasingly nearsighted (myopic). In its most advanced form, functional vision can be destroyed.[3]

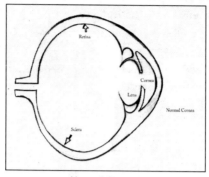

**Normal Cornea**

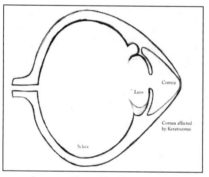

**Cornea affected by Keratoconus**

KC is not a common eye disease, and by no means is it rare. It has been estimated to occur in one out of every two thousand persons and its cause is not fully known. KC has its share of side effects, such as blurred vision, halos, blind spots, floaters, and other symptoms. Blurred vision is the loss of sharpness of vision and the inability to see small details. Blurred vision is enough by itself, and it robs a person with KC of a normal and quality sight life.

When I was diagnosed with KC, I didn't ask probing questions or attempt to dig in deep with research. Why? Basically, because I was in denial and my eye disease was treatable. I would be up in age before it would really cause me any serious concern. I had time, so why should I worry about something way on down the road?

Well, way on down the road came seven quick years later. With two new baby boys added to the household, I felt as though each new pregnancy was sucking away my eyesight. My eyesight was deteriorating rapidly. I had better come out of denial and deal with this challenge. You would think, right? No, I wasn't quite ready yet. KC was treatable, and my solace was that I was not yet "up in age."

· · · · ·

## Rigid Gas Permeable Contact Lenses (RGPs)

After about six months, my ophthalmologist found my case too challenging for his expertise. He referred me to the Southern College of Optometry. I was considered an excellent case study for KC. When I went to the Southern College of Optometry, I was wearing eyeglasses with extreme thickness around the curvature edges of each lens. I was taken out of eyeglasses and fitted for Rigid Gas Permeable (RGP) contact lenses. Most people who must wear RGPs are people with scarred, warped, or irregular corneas.

Rigid Gas Permeable contact lenses are custom-made, curved pieces of a durable, slightly flexible plastic shaped to fit your eyes. Because they transmit oxygen, these lenses are referred to as gas permeable, which allows the cornea to breathe. Oxygen is very important for the cornea to remain healthy. The original hard contact lens was made of a plastic that did not allow oxygen to reach the cornea and are rarely prescribed today. Since RGPs are rigid, they are also easier to handle, retain their shape over time, and provide crisper vision. Soft contacts are generally comfortable from the minute they are put on, but that isn't so with RGPs. Most wearers adjust to and become comfortable with RGPs, while some are not as tolerable of them and abandon wearing this type of contact lens altogether.

My RGP fittings were often long and exhausting. My eyes had become so well trained until I could sit through timely eye exams without blinking. Not only were the clinic's doctors and professors probing my eyes, but students also got their chance to look at my diseased corneas. I fondly started calling my eye care professionals at the college "Professor Doctors."

In order to wear RGPs, I would have to come back frequently for fittings until they could get the perfect fit. I was very apprehensive about having something in my eyes all day long. I was not looking forward to contact lenses at all, but this was the only option of treatment before me. Finally, that dreaded day arrived when I would have to wear the hard contact lenses.

As long as I live, I will never forget the first time that I saw the world through contact lenses. RGPs had enabled my vision to become well defined, clear, and sharp. Bearing through quite a timely adjustment period, my Professor Doctor finally let me leave. Happy for me and proud of his work, we walked outside together.

When I stepped outside, I was overwhelmed. I felt as though I had stepped into a vibrant oil painting. It was amazing how much of the world I hadn't been seeing clearly. With my new contact lenses, I felt born again. I could barely drive for taking in the sharp, bright images before me. Every word that came from my mouth praised God, and the angels in heaven were singing along with me. I was on a natural high and wouldn't have traded those contact lenses for anything.

Well, my life with RGPs was short-lived for that season. Just a few years later, another life-changing day presented itself when my Professor Doctor stated he could no longer treat my diseased corneas. My faithful RGPs were popping out because my corneas had coned beyond treatment. I could still tolerate an RGP in my left eye, but in order to see out of the right eye, I had reverted back to a pair of my stockpile eyeglasses. Simultaneously, I was wearing both eyeglasses and an RGP.

"Mrs. Nichols, your contact lens is sitting on your right cornea like a saucer sitting on top of a spiked edge. We've done all that we can do. It's time for you to have corneal transplants. I'm referring you to Dr. Thomas Wood, a specialist at the University of Tennessee Bowld Hospital."

Here I was at age thirty-five and yet again in a dazed state of mind as it pertained to my eyesight. I just couldn't believe that eyeglasses and hard contact lenses could not fix my vision problems.

"I'm supposed to be up in age before this happened to me," I cried to my trusted Professor Doctor. He looked just as awe-stricken as I felt while trying to explain how research was coming along for KC, and while in future years there would be more options than just corneal transplants, at this point, there was no more denying that I was functionally blind.

• • • • •

### Popeye to the Rescue

On my first visit to Dr. Thomas Wood's office, I felt out of place. The waiting room was filled with elderly patients with cataracts, glaucoma, and various eye conditions that they had lived with for years.

My elderly mother and father accompanied me on this

visit. My eyes were going to be dilated, and my father was going to drive me home. My mother was there to hold my hand. There was no need for my husband to take off work because my parents had always been a great support system during my years of fuzzy wuzzy vision. Plus, my father wanted to get a good understanding about my eye disease because his father had gone blind in his old age. Daddy was convinced that the doctor needed to know this pertinent information. Of course, my childhood memories of Papa Henry's blindness had been haunting me since my KC diagnosis.

When the nurse called my name to come into the exam room, she was expecting one of my parents to be the patient. Somewhat nervous and very apprehensive, I informed her that I was the one who couldn't see. Quickly, she calmed my fear and told me that Dr. Wood had a few other patients in my age group. I immediately took a liking to Dr. Wood during the examination. He came in, telling me how fuzzy wuzzy I was seeing.

"How do I look to you?" he asked me.

"You look like Popeye the Sailorman," I stated calmly. In my right mind, I never would have said that, but I was feeling depressed. He shouldn't have been my doctor because I wasn't "up in age" yet. However, like most folks that age, I spoke my mind.

He and his nurse laughed. "Hopefully, when I've completed your corneal transplants, I'll look much better to you. Young lady, we will revisit this conversation when you're seeing clearer."

Dr. Wood's bedside manner was quite refreshing, and he was just the kind of doctor that I needed. He was very humorous, and this was comforting. I felt blessed and trusted my eyes completely to his care. Dr. Wood confirmed to me and my parents that it was time for the transplants, but only one eye would be done. If the first transplant was successful, then we would have to wait one year before the second transplant would occur.

He then proceeded to write my name in a little black book, which he informed me was in his pocket at all times. He explained that I was on his shopping list for a donor match for my right cornea. To ensure donor compatibility, he would be looking for an African-American female within my same age range. Mainly, the donor would have to be dead and have donated their corneas for research through a national registry.

It all sounded so unreal. I couldn't believe that corneal transplants were the only corrective method of treatment. Surely, there were some eyeglasses or contact lenses out there for me. Years later, after I finally decided to dig deep and research KC, I learned about Boston Scleral lenses, which are specially designed and shaped to fit over the coned cornea for KC patients. But my destiny was corneal transplants. I wanted and needed the transplants, but at the same time, I just couldn't believe that it was going to happen to me.

Dr. Wood instructed me to go home and do my best at living as normal as I could with my one good contact lens and my assortment of eyeglasses. His words hit really hard when he said that there was nothing else he could do for me until a donor was found. I felt so helpless. I wanted him to fix my eyes and cure me immediately. I asked how long I would have to wait. He had no answer. I asked him what would happen if a donor was never found. I had so many questions of *what if,* but he just listened patiently and knowingly.

Finally, my tears came, and I wept uncontrollably. He assured my parents and me that he would become my personal Popeye the Sailorman and find me some eyes. Again, Dr. Wood's bedside manner calmed my fears. Without a doubt, I knew that he was the seasoned doctor that I'd been searching for and the vehicle that God would use to correct my diseased corneas.

• • • • •

## Blind As a Bat!

Nine months later, I was still waiting to hear from Dr. Wood. I had made only two calls to his office during that time and was reassured that I was not forgotten and my name was still in his little black book.

Living a normal life with my blurred vision was just about unbearable. My one good contact in my left eye finally stopped working, and I was totally dependent on my stockpile of thick prescription eyeglasses. I continued working an eight-hour job as a secretary to senior management, running my household with three school-age children, and active in the life of my church. At work, management modified my duties to overseeing the office and staff needs with limited clerical duties that required extreme visual attention. This was truly a blessing because I wanted to keep my job, and I needed the career side of my life to stay in tact. At home and church, let's just say that love covers a multitude of faults.

Although my immediate family was aware of my challenged and low vision, they really didn't know my full range of limitations. I didn't want them to know. I didn't want anyone to think that I had gone blind. The only persons who probably understood the full dynamics of my impaired vision were my husband and our young daughter. The boys were too young to fully grasp my limitations, but they knew I couldn't see. Plus, my parents and siblings felt that, like our grandfather Papa

Henry, blindness might just be my destiny. It was best that they didn't know the extent of my challenge.

During those nine months while waiting on a donor, God gave me angels and a double portion of humor and tolerance of my own self. Some of the things that happened to me were comical, and some were just downright frightening. The comical things were my everyday routine activities and the items that I just couldn't seem to see or find. The saying "If it had been a snake it would've bit me" should have been branded across my forehead. The frightening things had more to do with night vision, stairs, steps, and driving.

> "I kept my functional blindness as quiet as I could without putting it out there for everyone to know."

Now, I did have a few events that raised questions and suspicion to just how well I was really seeing. I had two near-fatal car accidents. I broke my ankle from a fall and wore a cast for ten weeks. I acquired bruises from falling up or down steps and stairs and from bumping or walking into things. I acquired a few cuts, scalds, and burns from cooking and ironing. Basic things like reading and especially reading in public, watching television, going to the movies, journaling, decorating, cleaning house, sightseeing, and traveling were no longer fun to do. They all required too much squinting and effort to see. It was a sad day when I had to admit that my driving privileges had to cease if I wanted to continue living.

Surprisingly, these things I could handle, but sympathy and depression I wanted nowhere near me. It was truly amazing how God carried me during my season of being functionally blind. You can also say that I became a stand-up comedian during that season. I had to keep myself laughing to keep from crying.

There were times that God empowered my eyes and I could see reasonably well with my assortment of eyeglasses, and then there were times I couldn't see past the tip of my nose. The well-known reading *Footprints* took on a new meaning to my life. To this day, I keep a framed poster-sized artwork of it hanging in my writing room. I know for certain that God carried me and gave me a special anointing for that unbearable fuzzy wuzzy season in my life.

• • • • •

### The Surgery: Penetrating Keratoplasty (PK)

On that life-changing Mother's Day in 1991, after receiving Dr. Wood's call, it was finally time for corneal transplant surgery. I had been waiting nine months for him to find a donor. The nine months became quite symbolic as I pondered over the *whys* of my life. I felt like I was being created again, but this time outside of the womb. God was recreating me while teaching, molding, pruning, and polishing me for his divine purposes. I was a work in progress. And to this day, he is still preparing me for his kingdom's purposes.

Matthew 5:29 says, if your right eye offends you—pluck it out and cast it from you. Well, that is exactly the way I felt when it was time for me to have my first corneal transplant. My right cornea was giving me the blues, and it had to go.

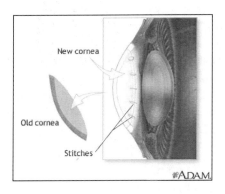

Corneal transplant surgery involves removing the diseased cornea surgically and replacing it with a donated cornea. This operation is also called corneal graft surgery or penetrating keratoplasty. Statistics state that only twenty to twenty-five percent of those with KC ultimately require corneal transplant surgery. Only the front transparent portion of the eye, the cornea, is transplanted. The whole eye is not transplanted. A corneal transplant is the way of removing your damaged cornea and replacing it with a healthy cornea from the eye of a suitable donor. [4]

Surgery can be a crucial and sometimes frightening decision. However, those who know what to expect before, during, and after surgery are better prepared for the experience. Dr. Wood had explained the surgery process, and I knew fully well what was ahead of me. That is why I had to properly plan for my family's care before and after the surgery.

When I checked into one-day surgery, I was wired up. I had been busy making arrangements for my children's transportation to and from school, done a week's worth of laundry, and made sure that there were plenty of groceries in the house. I went to work bright and early to delegate assignments for that week's staff conference.

Of course, I was apprehensive about the surgery, but my coping mechanism was to keep busy and to not think about it. At the hospital, there was another young African-American woman in the preparation room. I was certain that she was receiving the left cornea. True enough, she was. She told me that this would be Dr. Wood's second attempt at finding the right donor for her. Her first corneal transplant was rejected by her body. She was more nervous and apprehensive than I was.

My husband stayed with me as long as they would let him. He was advised to go home, and Dr. Wood would call him when it was time to come pick me up. After he left, I really felt all alone. Dr. Wood had advised that I would be fully awake. He explained that he needed my eye muscles working while he did the surgery. I would be given a mild sedative to keep me calm.

I was rolled into an area where I was prepped for surgery. I caught a glimpse of a table lined with long surgical tools. It didn't take me long to assess that the majority of them looked like needles of various lengths and sizes. Undoubtedly, it was time for another sedative when I realized these instruments were going to be used on me. Dr. Wood patiently and calmly explained that I could bear the needles. I trusted him completely because, after all, he was my Popeye the Sailorman.

I imagined myself being in the dentist's chair as the needles deadened the area around my eye. And believe it or not, I saw every needle that was used as it invaded my eye cavity. Talk about mind over matter; I had to apply everything in my psyche to stay calm and let the mild sedative do its job.

However, I knew in my heart that it was the Holy Spirit calming me.

After the initial deadening and feeling as though I had been stroke induced along the right side of my face, I was draped with facial surgical coverings. My right eye remained exposed for more needles and the actual transplant process. Dr. Wood explained everything he was doing step-by-step. There were no sudden surprises or unexplained moves. I could feel pressure as he indicated, but other than that, it was a smooth operation.

In the operating room, Dr. Wood had soft classical musical playing in the background. He was very relaxed, as were the people assisting him. Surprisingly, I was glad that I was awake during the surgery. Toward the end, my husband was called so that we could all talk over the speaker telephone. It was really cool. He and the children were eating dinner, and I was able to speak with them while lying on the operating table. Dr. Wood encouraged him to take his time to get the children down for the evening before coming to get me.

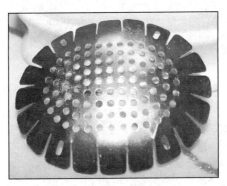

As they prepared me to go home, it was I who felt like Popeye the Sailorman with the bandage and aluminum shield covering my eye. Equipped with eye drops, ointment, and instructions for care, I went home rejoicing and ready to accept whatever challenges lay ahead. The aftercare was my biggest concern, but after a few days, it ceased to bother me. I slept in the aluminum shield at night for a period of time to protect the corneal graft. When going outside, I had several pairs of those big black sunglasses that are commonly worn after eye surgeries.

My healing process was normal with no complications. However, I did experience loose sutures (stitches). Most patients' sutures are removed after a year by the doctor and in his office. This was not my fate. Sutures can loosen and cause a foreign body feeling, especially when you blink. The loose suture can easily be removed but only in the doctor's office with tweezers.

In my case, once the stitches started coming loose, they were popping out like popcorn. It was very uncomfortable and painful. There was a constant scratching and burning to my eyelids. I had quite a few after-hour and weekend visits to see Dr. Wood or whoever was on call to pluck the loose suture out of my eye. Dr. Wood assured me that my eye was healing properly and the corneal graft was safe.

I experienced immediate benefits from my new corneal graft. I still had quite a bit of astigmatism in the right eye, but my right eye had become my strongest eye. Even though my vision was still challenged, it was better than its previous condition. My left cornea would just have to wait its turn to be plucked out.

It was a year before Dr. Wood put me back into a rigid gas permeable lens for the right eye only. With my new corneal graft and my one new RGP lens, I was seeing much better than I had ever seen in my right eye since the KC diagnosis. Technically, I was still functionally blind with such low vision in my left eye, but to me I was seeing perfectly.

One year after the right corneal transplant, I was back on Dr. Wood's shopping list for the left cornea. I waited about six months before a donor was found for the second transplant. Again, the procedure went like clockwork. Unfortunately, I experienced the unpleasant saga of loose sutures and endured once again another plucking-out process until complete healing was obtained. I waited another year before Dr. Wood put me into a new RGP for the left eye. Once again, I was fully equipped with two RGPs and back to celebrating contact lenses as my best friends for life.

I'm sure you're thinking that the transplants should have corrected my low and challenged vision. In one aspect it most certainly did because by no means is my sight as bad off as it was prior to corneal transplants. For once, I could see clearer than I had seen in my entire life, but I still need RGPs, which are truly my best visual aids and companions.

• • • • •

## *Gear Up to See*

Once upon a time, I thought that contact lenses were for cosmetic purposes only—especially for those who didn't want to have the four-eyed look. That was until I discovered that I couldn't see without them. For KCers, contact lenses are the equivalent of a seeing-eye dog. Today, I wouldn't dare think of living without a pair or two and all the paraphernalia that comes along with them.

The process of gearing up to see is a daily and disciplined routine. Before corneal transplants, I used to apply more time putting on eye makeup. But that time is now allocated to making sure my contact lenses are cleaned and disinfected before putting them on. Since corneal transplants, I use eye makeup very sparingly. KCers cannot afford to let anything infect, irritate, or damage their corneal grafts. At the end of each day, it is equally important to establish a disciplined routine for the removal, cleaning, and storing of the contact lens for healthy maintenance and longevity.

Dry eye syndrome, blinking, winking, facial twitching, and weakened eye muscles all come in the package deal with prolonged contact lens use. So when you see me, know that I'm either having a good eye day or a bad eye day. You'll be able to tell by the teary appearance, winking, and/or constant blinking of my eyes. Just smile and know that I'm truly blessed and favored by the Lord.

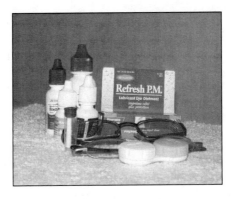

This is a photo of my personal items that are kept in a cherished black bag, which is in my possession at all times. It contains my rigid gas permeable lenses (RGPs), cleaning solution, disinfectant, Patanol eye drops, rewetting drops, Refresh PM, a lens suction removal stick, reading glasses, and a pair of prescription eyeglasses. The only thing not photographed is my sunglasses. At one time, I was wearing only prescription sunglasses, but now I wear regular ultraviolet protective sunglasses found in retail stores.

• • • • •

## The Blessing

Since that day of KC diagnosis and to this very day, I've had to rise above the emotional pain and fearful thoughts of immobility, depression, isolation, being alone, and failure. I've learned to replace those feelings with much more positive and spiritual thinking. I had to have a positive and hopeful attitude if I wanted to survive and to do what I had to do to make each day count. God has given me life, a full and blessed life. My life is certainly worth living simply by just living it the way he has created, purposed, and destined it.

Perhaps you have also been diagnosed with an illness or are enduring a difficult circumstance that has caused you to draw nearer to our Heavenly Father. It is through our life's challenges that God performs his continued and best work in molding and shaping our lives. Truly, God is the potter, and we are the clay. By no means does your disease, illness, or circumstance totally define you as a person, but it is certainly a viable part of your life. It's how you choose to handle it that determines who you are and shapes your destiny.

I thank God for blessing me with KC. KC has allowed me to grow, to change, to understand, to live my life purposes, and to enter into a deeper relationship with him.

> My brethren, count it all joy when ye fall into diverse temptations; Knowing [this], that the trying of your faith worketh patience. But let patience have [her] perfect work, that ye may be perfect and entire, wanting nothing. If any of you lack wisdom, let him ask of God, that giveth to all [men] liberally, and upbraideth not; and it shall be given him. But let him ask in faith, nothing wavering. For he that wavereth is like a wave of the sea driven with the wind and tossed. James 1:1–6

My dear friends, I say with much conviction, "Whatever betides you, count it all as joy!" Say and sing in your heart, "It is well, it is well, with my soul."

# How Is Your Vision?

"The question is not what you
look at but what you see."
–Henry David Thoreau–[5]

Eye exams are important. Most people do not think about getting an eye exam until they start to experience vision problems. Getting regular eye examinations are crucial to preserving eye health and maintaining excellent vision.

It's important that you don't confuse vision screening at health fairs, office clinics, and other forums with a comprehensive eye examination. You want an exam that will check for more than just 20/20 vision measured by how well you see the letters on an eye chart. A comprehensive eye examination will check for visual skills, eye disorders, and diseases that have no early symptoms.

After my second transplant in 1993, my two new corneal grafts, rigid gas permeable contact lenses, and a pair of prescription glasses carried me for seven years. The fact that I went for seven years without seeing an eye care doctor was remarkable. Sadly, the day came when my sacred visual aides began to fail me.

Well, what did I expect? I was expecting them to last forever because I had claimed healing. Biblically, the number seven represents perfection or completion, and that was a good sign. God was confirming my healing because his healing through two new corneal grafts was perfect. However, I thank God for giving me the good sense to know that if I wanted to continue to see better, I had best get new visual aids.

A KCer's eye care professional is worth silver and gold. That's why it is so important that the patient-physician relationship is in tact. It's enough that the KCer's world is already fuzzy wuzzy, and a doctor who knows and understand the challenges of KC will exercise the patience and efficiency in diagnosing, treating, and lens fitting of the KC patient. If your eye care professional doesn't meet this expectation, then I strongly recommend that you dismiss him or her and find another.

> "No matter what the sickness or illness, not only do you require but you deserve the best professional health care possible."

The following statements are from my latest eye care professionals. First, I must admit that I never bothered to ask, remember, or understand all of the specifics associated with my vision. Thus, I will not be able to give you the clinical dimensions of my once-upon-a-time diseased corneas. All I know is that my KC was an advanced case.

• • • • •

## *Peter B. Benvenuto, O.D., F.A.A.O.,*
## *Memphis, Tennessee*

Mrs. Nichols was first seen in our offices in February 2000. She reported that she had corneal transplants in each eye in the early nineties secondary to keratoconus. Her exams at that time showed her to be a compound mytopic astigmat in the right eye and a compound hyperopic astigmat in the left eye with clear grafts in each eye and no topographic evidence of keratoconus. Up until this year, Mrs. Nichols was wearing custom astigmatic soft contact lenses and seeing with adequate vision. This year she has shown an increase in astigmatic error but still no topographic evidence of keratoconus. We are currently trying to fit her with Bi-toric rigid gas permeable lenses.

• • • • •

## *Dr. Artee D. Nanji, O.D., Memphis, Tennessee*

Mrs. Nichols was first seen in our office in July 2006. She reported that she had corneal transplants in the early nineties due to keratoconus. She was seen in our office because her last pair of glasses prescribed by Dr. Benvenuto had been damaged and out of adjustment. At that time, she was seeing 20/100 in both the right and left eye. On that visit, I was able to correct her to 20/50 in the right eye but not the left eye. In order to correct the left eye, I requested the records from Dr. Benvenuto and had her come in for a prescription recheck. At her follow-up visit, I was able to correct her vision to 20/70 in the right eye, 20/40 in the left eye, and

20/30 in both eyes. She was given a prescription and recommended that she follow up with a corneal evaluation and topography to ensure that her grafts were stable.

•  •  •  •  •

### *Dr. Nicole M. Mills, O.D., Low Vision Resident–Southern College of Optometry, Memphis, Tennessee*

Mrs. Nichols was seen at Clovernook Center for the Blind and Visually Impaired for a low vision evaluation in January 2008. At that time, Mrs. Nichols was reporting that she was wearing her RGP contact lenses less and less due to decreased comfort throughout the day. Since the contact lenses provided better vision for her over glasses, I had to ensure that I found a spectacle prescription that would offer her the best possible vision she could achieve with glasses. I found both eyes were hyperopic (far-sighted) with very high amounts of astigmatism correction needed to provide her with 10/20 Feinbloom vision in both eyes (equivalent to 20/40 Snellen vision in both eyes). Her spectacle prescription is: OD: +1.50–10.00x047; OS: +1.25–8.50x147; Add: +1.50. Not only did I prescribe glasses, but I found that two low vision devices helped aid Mrs. Nichols in achieving her goals of improving her vision for reading and working on the computer. A 3.5x LED-illuminated, hand-held magnifier was found to be very beneficial for her for near spotting tasks, and Eschenbach's MaxDetail glasses worked very well for reading & working on the computer.

------

"Have you had your eyes checked, lately?"

------

Now, I ask you the question, "What does your eye care professional say about your eyes?" Perhaps you are fortunate enough not to have any eye problems. But as my parents would say with much passion and conviction, "just keep on living." The aging process will certainly bring changes to your eyesight. During regular exams, your doctor will check for vision problems, glaucoma, cataracts, macular degeneration, and diabetes-related eye conditions. If you notice any sudden changes in your vision, go see your doctor right away. These changes could indicate a more serious condition.

Don't neglect your gift of sight or take it for granted. Your eyes have been there for you all these years, performing the miraculous conversion of light to sight. Making it seem as if it's no big deal. But if your vision ever does start to go, you can be certain that you will miss it dearly. So take care of your sight. Take steps to nurture it and to ensure that your sight will last your lifetime.

# Do You See What I See?

"If you go as far as you can see,
you will then see enough to go even farther."
–John Wooden–[6]

As in the above quote, when my vision was at its lowest and most challenged, I would go as far as I could see, and when I got to that end point there was always more ahead for me to see things a little bit better and to go a little bit farther. John Wooden also stated, "Do not let what you can't do interfere with what you can do." Although my vision wasn't the best, I never let it stop me from doing what I could do and living a full, well-balanced life.

KC teaches you how to adapt but not to surrender. You learn to live, cope, and persevere to higher heights. It's not until you're without something that you realize how it affects your quality of life. At different stages in my KC progression, I began to live with continuous limitations. Most KCers adapt to living with KC as being an annoying nuisance that hinders a normal, healthy sight life.

I was once an avid reader, and it was devastating not to

see the text clearly on pages. The pleasure of watching television was no longer enjoyable because of the need to squint my eyes to see a clear picture. I credit KC with giving me the discipline of writing because it was easier for me to type with my eyes closed than watch television or read books.

As my KC progressed, recognizing faces, facial expressions, and hand movements, from a moderate distance, became increasingly impossible. First, I barely could see the person to even recognize who they were and to do any lip reading, see facial gestures, and hand signals were totally nonexistent. You would've had to been standing within arm's reach for me to see you, and still there was no guarantee that I could see the fine details of your face and other items.

After both my corneal transplants, it was indeed a pleasure and eye opener to see faces that I hadn't seen clearly in years. Some KCers have expressed the thrill of seeing their own facial freckles after corneal transplant surgery.

The art and skill of housecleaning became difficult and depressing. Keeping a clean house is already a task. My vision became so poor that soon I couldn't see obvious stains, dust, and dirt in my own home. Decorating and hanging wallpaper became something that I used to do. I went through the motions of cleaning and hoped that my house was at least halfway presentable. Eventually, I quit inviting friends over and having overnight guests. As an example of how my KC eyes see, take the beige Formica countertops in my kitchen. Within the design, there are subtle elements of green and bronze speckles. I see only a solid beige countertop. My KC eyes cannot see the fine intricate details of anything.

Something as personal as styling my hair and putting on makeup became time consuming and exhausting. It was of necessity that I cut my hair and wore a short stylish cut at all times. Makeup was not a major requirement because God had blessed me with a youthful face and natural beauty attributes. Eye concealer for the dark circles around my eyes, a powder sponge, and lipstick was about all that I could manage.

Daytime driving was a necessity and reasonably safe, but nighttime driving was like playing Russian roulette. In 1985, before corneal transplant surgeries, my driver's license expired the same month that I gave birth to our second child. I had good intentions of renewing as soon as I had time. Surprisingly, six months later, I was pregnant again. Shortly thereafter, with a preschooler and two baby boys, I was an emotional and psychological wreck. During that time, my KC was progressing rapidly. I had narrowed my daytime driving on an expired license within a twenty-mile radius from home, work, the children's school and daycare, church, and to my parent's home. I stopped driving at night completely. More and more, I procrastinated on getting a new driver's license because it would require passing the eye test at the Department of Motor Vehicles.

On one of my needed driving outings with the children to my parent's home, I was pulled over by a police officer. He listened to my sad story, and then proceeded to report my expired license to dispatch, while not issuing me a ticket. He strongly advised me to make sure that the DMV was my major outing on the following day. The next day at the DMV, by the grace of God and with two pair of eyeglasses, it was a struggle and I barely passed the dreaded eye examination. I vowed that if I had to ever visit the DMV again that it would not be due to an expired driver's license.

The list of limitations that persons with KC experience on a daily basis goes on and on. From sports and recreational activities to professional and technical careers, which rely on strong visual acuity, is hindered and in some cases abandoned. By no means should KC be taken lightly by its victims or the world at large.

Can you imagine having sight but not being able to see things clearly? Perhaps, you can on a temporary or short-term basis. But imagine seeing this way every day, for years and years, not improving but with progressive deterioration. How do KCers feel about living with this debilitating eye disease? I'm positive that I express the sentiments of worldwide KCers in the next statement.

> "Having KC is irritating, an inconvenience, and a downright nuisance!"

Do this quick exercise with me. Take a look around the room that you're in. Blink your eyes and look again. Notice how the various images and colors that you see update quickly and constantly as you blink. We know this amazing function of the eyes and brain working together as the sense of sight. Truly, this natural camera within the human body is amazing.

My husband has a 35mm Minolta camera. The high-quality lens can zoom in on an object and will flash only if in focus. If not in focus, it clicks and clicks but doesn't complete the process. You have to shoot from a different angle to finally acquire a picture. A KCer's eyes are processing like that 35mm camera when it's trying to get a clear image. This is the fate of KCers and a vast majority of persons living with challenged vision.

Visionally speaking, normal-sighted persons without KC process objects quicker and clearer. However, KCers' eyes need a minute or two to pause, adjust, and read, just before processing what has been seen. The final view can range from obscure, to abstract, or to nonexistent. It's very similar to having a good or bad hair day. KCers have good and bad eye days. We may or may not see what you see. It's not that KCers cannot see, but what we see is blurred and out of focus.

One of the many challenges for a KCer is to explain the quality of sight experienced. You know it's bad when the big "E" on the eye chart appears to be a big smudge on the wall. To see the letterings thereafter can become a skillful game at just plain guessing. Because I'm not legally blind, people think that I can see as clearly as they can especially if I'm wearing eyeglasses or contact lenses. Sometimes I tell them about my challenged vision, and sometimes I don't. No matter how distorted and unfocused it appears, I just let them think I see what they see.

The expression "picture this" opens your mind to see what someone else sees and tap into their perspective. You would think that people see the same thing when looking at the same object, right? But it is always amazing how people can see the same thing but each one has a different viewpoint about what was seen.

Take, for instance, your particular challenge or situation. You may see it as devastating or life threatening. Another person may see it being not as bad as what they are dealing with. But from the eyes of God, he sees it as a life giving and soul saving opportunity. Ultimately, your outcome is going to depend on how you see your challenge and how you respond to it. I see God's gift of purpose, healing, and salvation for my life in having KC.

The following picture may help you see from the eyes of a person with KC or any person that lives with challenged vision. As they say, a picture is worth a thousand words.

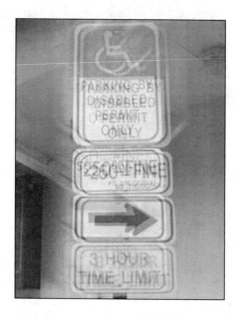

*Keratoconus often results in monocular double vision, in which a person sees multiple images in each eye. This example of how the world appears to a keratoconus patient can be found at KCVision, an online visual reference source for patients and families. Visit the link at http://kcvision.org [7]*

# What Is Your Diagnosis?

"Whatever we expect with confidence becomes
our own self-fulfilling prophecy."
-Brian Tracy- [8]

One of the surest things that can turn your world upside down
is a devastating diagnosis. Confusion, fear, sadness, hopeless-
ness, and seeming as though you're on an emotional seesaw are
common feelings when the doctor gives you bad news.

I'm positive that when you're diagnosed with any type of
disease or illness, it's not something that you want to hear or
live with. I also feel that when you embrace that diagnosis,
whether it is positive or negative, it determines your quality
of life and future existence.

It is my belief that another part of your life's journey
begins the day you receive a life-changing diagnosis. Take a
few minutes and focus on your situation or diagnosis. How
did you feel when you heard the words coming from the
doctor's mouth or whoever delivered what seemed to be
your future life sentencing? Did you feel like you may as

well lie down and die? Or did you feel what was said didn't determine the course for your life's direction?

I felt the latter. I didn't care what the doctor had said. I refused to believe that God would take away my eyesight. This attitude might have been denial, but the deeper truth of the matter was that my faith was stronger than the diagnosis. I wasn't ready to deal with living my life as a person with limited and challenged vision. Maybe, when I was old and gray, I could accept it better. Besides, most old folk couldn't see well anyway. This is how I consoled myself upon being diagnosed with KC.

> **"What did you do or say to console yourself?"**

In retrospect, I should have asked more questions and done some research about KC. For sure, my knowledge base about KC would be more than it is today. If I had started researching and writing twenty-five years ago, I would be on top of my game when it comes to knowing all there is to know about KC, right? Probably so, but it didn't happen that way. I'm so thankful that it has taken these twenty-five years for God to groom, process, and make the best of me.

Somewhere I read that the acronym for fear means *False Evidence Appearing Real.* I'll be the first to admit that fear became alive and in full effect as I realized that my eyesight wasn't going to get any better but worse. I had been treated by several optometrists, an ophthalmologist, and Professor Doctors at the eye college, and an eye surgeon. Yes, the evidence before me was very real, and the diagnosis was true, and I was scared.

Since being diagnosed with KC, I've learned some basic truths about fear. Humorously, the real four-letter *F* word is *fear.* It should be taken out of our vocabularies when it pertains to truth and deliverance. Fear is the greatest obstacle to overcoming day-to-day problems. We conquer fears by facing them and by taking action. A lack of knowledge creates fear, but the best remedy for fear is information. And most importantly, "God has not given us the spirit of fear but of power and love and a strong mind" (2 Timothy 1:7).

What did I do with my fear? Did I face my fear and take action when diagnosed with KC? My answer is *no* because I decided to post-pone dealing with the big picture and I chose to live with the short-range approach and hoped that my KC would not progress. Where did that get me? It's gotten me to where I am today. Now, twenty-five years later, I'm taking action by digging in deep, researching what new and innovated treatments are available for KCers, writing a book, starting a support group, and continuing to live my life one day at a time with a modified level of challenged vision.

It's senseless to question the what-ifs in life. So don't beat yourself up if you've been in a mode of denial or hiding your head in the sand; it's part of the process. It truly depends on what you're dealing with and the time parameters of your diagnosis. The sooner you open your mind to its truth, the quicker you will respond and equip yourself with knowledge and information.

If you've been diagnosed with any illness, disease, or going through an unbearable situation, I advise you to learn all that you can about your illness and the truth about your matter. Ask questions and discuss your concerns with your doctor and others. Find a support group dealing with the same illness or problem. Start a support group yourself if one is not available in your area. A support system will be both enlightening and reassuring.

Since childhood, I've experienced and watched family members and others respond to difficult diagnoses and medical crises. It is through these experiences that I've learned how to get through the emotion-filled days of any diagnosis. When you first hear the news, it seems as if life is never going to be the same or normal again. But amazingly, our minds and spirits incorporate the diagnosis into our being, and we handle it. Day by day you learn to adjust, cope, do what is needed, and go on to the next process.

There is no right or perfect way to respond to any diagnosis. People respond and cope in different ways. You will find the coping skills that work best for you based on how you solve problems and manage stress. However, it is vitally important that you use and learn healthy, effective coping skills. Generally, those who cope successfully have strong support systems. They have open communication with those who care and have confidence in their healthcare providers.

There are many ways to reduce and manage stress. Learn what works for you and find new techniques that you haven't tried. The following categories list my core methods for handling difficult matters. Each category gives me a base for coping, acceptance, and moving on. Begin to utilize each method into your life, and I guarantee you'll see a difference.

*Inhale & Exhale:* Inhale and take in everything that has happened. Determine the things that you can control as well as the things that are out of your control. Make a choice and decide to conquer or be conquered. Now, exhale. Choose to accept and live one day at a time.

*Reach Upward:* Now is the time when you will discover where you are spiritually. You'll discover if your prayer life is existent or nonexistent. Since creation, man has practiced prayer. You may feel that prayer is a useless ritual with no evidence of results. No matter what you may think about prayer—it works!

*Reach Inward:* Draw on your inner strength. Believe me, it is there. Once you tap into it, you'll be amazed at your own fortitude and survival instincts. Give yourself positive self-talk of healing, encouragement, and spiritual nourishment from God's word.

*Reach Out:* Talk about how you feel. Draw from the strength of family and loved ones. Connect with a support group that can identify with your situation. The best information can be found from those who have experienced and those who are going through the same circumstances.

Finally, there is no doubt that a negative diagnosis changes people's lives. The emotional stress it causes can be overwhelming. Be assured that it is normal to feel fearful, sad, and frustrated. Remember, no man is an island, and you don't have to go through it alone. Most importantly, accepting the diagnosis and incorporating it into your life is an ongoing process. Expect to meet your diagnosis or devastating situation with confidence, and you will be significantly successful in making decisions and impacting your quality of life.

# Is It a Problem or a Challenge?

"People only see what they are prepared to see."
–Ralph Waldo Emerson–[9]

Oftentimes, I ask the question, "What's the difference between a problem and a challenge?" Think about it. Everybody has problems—big ones and small ones. Problems slow us down, drain and block our energy, and leave us undecided or confused.

I think the answer to the question is in the view you decide to take. Whether you view a situation as a problem or a challenge does not make the situation go away, does it? But your view does influence your attitude and the actions you take.

It's taken me some years, but I've learned to view any circumstance or situation that I meet as either "difficult" or "favorable." The view of my problem now defines the level of my challenge and the actions that I'll take.

A problem can be viewed as any question or matter involving doubt, uncertainty, or difficulty. The word challenge can be viewed as an invitation to compete in a fight, contest, or competition. Put the two definitions together and ask yourself, "How do I choose to fight this difficulty?"

Now ask, "What is my problem? How will this problem serve me, work for me, move me forward, and give me positive energy?"

Can you see how a difficult situation is now an invitation to compete? Now, you should be inspired to take actions that will significantly influence the outcome that you will experience.

> "Do you face your problems as challenges?"

Zoom in on the aforementioned questions and give yourself the "for real" answers. You have to get to the root cause of what it is that is causing you to have pain, discomfort, or an unbearable existence.

Is it health related? Is it a matter of being heart-broken? Is it causing life to pass you by? As long as you are denying the reality and the truth about your situation, then you see only what you want to see. Maybe that's all you're prepared to see and want to see at that time. But to have divine liberation, you have to see it the way it really appears in its truest form.

My KC problem literally had to do with how I was seeing through my eyes. It took a few years after the initial diagnosis to accept that this problem was taking away my eyesight. Was I going to fret, worry, and complain? How would I fight this difficult matter?

Eventually, I decided that I may have KC, but KC didn't have me. Even though the diseased corneas have been removed through corneal transplants, I still have to live with low vision concerns.

I have chosen to fight, compete, and do whatever it takes

to work around, over and above my low vision. If it takes more surgery, utilizing visual aide tools for the blind, taking on a more intense daily regime of eye care, then that is what I'm going to do; whatever it takes! My low vision problem has become a challenge, and when challenged, the overall desire is to win.

This whole mental process of turning problems into challenges is a series of taking charge. As you take charge of life's problems, diagnoses, medical processes, and treatments, realize that daily efforts and focused goals will help you succeed.

- Have a very clear idea of how your situation is going to change. Feel it and know it with all your senses as if you have already achieved it.

- Discover your strengths and weaknesses during the process.

- Bring yourself back on track when distracted or discouraged.

- Refocus, start over, and begin again when necessary.

- Measure your progress by how far you have come, not by how far you still have to go.

- Remember that it's no longer a problem; it's a challenge, and challenges can be conquered.

# Why Me?

"Pain and love—the whole of life, in short—cannot be
looked on as a disease just because they make us suffer."
–Italo Svevo–[10]

Have you ever asked, "Lord, why did you allow this to happen to me?" I would be telling an untruth if I said I never asked that question. If you're looking to have a crying session or pity party, then surely that question will get you off to a good start. Look around you and you'll see that most people, if not everyone, have been dealt a short straw or two in their lives. God gets our attention in different ways.

For some it is a handicap or disability. It could be an enemy. It could be loneliness. It could be unhappy living conditions. It could be a chronic illness or physical condition. For some it may be unemployment or underemployment. But one thing is for certain; if you have thorns in your life, then thank God for the roses that surrounds them.

If you're asking, *Why me?* for truth and revelation, the answer is quite clear. Think about Jesus Christ and his life here on earth. Jesus was God's only Son, yet he had to endure his plight to the end. If anyone had the right to ask *Why me?* Jesus would be first on the list.

In the Garden of Gethsemane, Jesus did ask for the cup to be removed from him if possible. Like you and me, Jesus had his moments of despair, but he didn't wallow in it. Within that same setting, he said, "Oh, my Father, nevertheless, not my will but your will be done." Jesus understood that Calvary was his destiny and that he had to drink of this cup for God's divine plan to be fulfilled. Read and study Matthew 26:34–45.

Now, if Jesus had to bear his diagnosis, prognosis, or circumstance, where does that leave us? Think about it! I finally changed the question into, "Lord, why not me?"

Since he is my creator and Heavenly Father, he knew that I could handle KC. God knows that you can handle that which he has put on your life's plate. Just as God answered Paul in 2 Corinthians 12:9, "And he said unto me, my grace is sufficient for thee." God says the same to you and me. God's grace is sufficient for every area of our life. It is sufficient to save us. It is sufficient to secure us. It is sufficient to strengthen us.

Our lives do not always go as we plan, wish, or dream. Life is known for throwing good and bad curveballs. The ability to accept and let go is the way to deal with unexpected illnesses, situations, and turns of fate. Curveballs are life's way of keeping us awake, and they can bring us wonderful surprises and discoveries about ourselves. So the next time life hands you a curveball, take a deep breath, say thank you, and open your mind to a new opportunity.

"How are you handling your curveballs?"

I recommend that you find a scripture, motto, or slogan that will apply to your circumstance. Commit it to memory and confirm its affirmation in your life daily. Life and death are in the power of the tongue. Speak life and you will immediately see the benefits of its transforming power to your mental, emotional, and spiritual well-being.

For years, I had read the Serenity Prayer, but I never applied it to circumstances in my life. "God grant me the serenity to accept the things I cannot change, the courage to change the things I can, and the wisdom to know the difference." Wow, what power and simplicity exist in this short prayer! Truly, there are life-changing affirmations that lie within this universal prayer.

There was nothing that I could do to change my KC diagnosis. With each passing year, the evidence of my deteriorating sight was undeniable. KC was going to take me on a journey whether I wanted to go or not. I needed courage to face my future. What I could change was how I was going to let it affect my attitude and well-being. Once the courage kicked in to accept my KC condition, the wisdom to learn all about it and to live with its daily challenges became more tolerable and accepted.

# Am I Healed?

"If you want to heal the body, you
must first heal the mind."
- Plato -[II]

Since receiving two corneal transplants and seeing pretty well for the past sixteen years, I considered myself healed. I had to ask myself, *If I still have to wear specialty rigid gas permeable contact lenses (RGPs), am I truly healed?* My answer to that is *yes!* My corneal grafts are disease free, and I'm not considered functionally blind anymore. Sounds like healing to me!

---

"Have you ever questioned your healing?"

---

A few months ago, I had to seriously ponder over the above question. I was experiencing fuzzy wuzzy vision again. *Has my KC come back? What happened to my healing? Lord, surely I'm not about to face being functionally blind again?* Reluctantly, I made the dreaded visit to my eye doctor. After testing, he stated that my corneal grafts were still looking healthy after sixteen years, and that I needed a new RGP prescription.

So I ask myself again, *Am I healed?* My answer is still a firm *yes!* I believe the healing came in the form of my two new corneal grafts. I had to remind myself that the diseased corneas had been plucked out and I've been able to alternate between eyeglasses and contact lenses. In my opinion, I am no different from a normal sighted person that uses visual aids.

Am I saying I don't have KC anymore? Does that mean I'm at a stage where KC has ceased progression? What I'm saying with certainty is that I live with "residuals" of KC. Residuals can be defined as something that remains to discomfort or disable a person following an illness, injury, or operation. I have remnants of my original limitations but nowhere as severe as the advanced symptoms of KC. I may have KC issues after corneal transplants, but KC doesn't have me!

Proverbs 23:7 says for as a man thinks in his heart, so is he. At this very moment you are who you think you are. You have what you think you deserve. You are the manifestation of the constant processing of your thoughts. I've received what God has provided for me, and that was two new healthy corneas. Although I live with challenged vision, I live a normal, healthy, and sighted life just as anyone else.

Have you allowed a diagnosis, prognosis, or any circumstance to rob you of an emotional, physical, or spiritual healing? My recommendation is to change what you think, and you will change your entire life.

> "What have you allowed to rob you of your healing?"

Ask yourself, "What negativity have I allowed to become acceptable in my life?" If you think and meditate on a negative diagnosis or circumstance, you will become what it says. However, if you meditate on God's Word, you will become like a tree planted by rivers of living waters that brings forth fruitful evidence in all seasons of your life.

Have you heard the expression, "First comes the dealing then the healing." Think about it. Deal with what you have no matter what it is. Stop complaining and learn to live with it. Yes, turn your lemons into lemonade.

One way to appreciate your situation is to think of the pain of others who are suffering from illnesses, diagnoses, prognoses, and life challenges more so devastating than your own situation. With this perspective, your situation doesn't appear so bad in comparison, right? It's okay to allow yourself to feel what you're feeling, but don't wallow and stay there.

I believe that God wants us well and that he will heal us if it's his will for our lives. He's provided us with doctors and medical technology to perform miraculous outcomes, and I thank God for them. Go to the doctor. Attend a support group. Talk to somebody. Go get yourself some help. Had it not been for doctors and technology, I wouldn't be able to say, "I was once blind, but now I see."

Now that I've reshaped my thinking about KC and decreeing that I am healed, I'm more desirous than ever to live a healthier lifestyle. KC has given me a purpose to live my life to its fullest. In essence, my challenge became my lifeline. Through better nutrition, exercise, relaxation, sleep, and so much more, I'm going to benefit emotionally, physically, and spiritually.

I encourage you to take off the blinders and see a clearer picture of what life has handed you. No matter how dismal or challenging it may be, embrace it, accept it, and live life to the fullest. You might just discover God's unique and divine plan for your life.

# Do You Have Spiritual Eyes?

"Open thou mine eyes that I may behold
wondrous things out of thy law."
Psalms 119:18 [12]

What are your thoughts on having spiritual eyes? Can seeing things from a spiritual perspective help your circumstance, situation, or diagnosis? I believe that within each of us there is a capacity for vision beyond the natural eyesight.

Every human being has spiritual eyes, but we must use them. God gave them to us so that we could apprehend the spiritual realities of life. We must learn to see things as God sees them. When we see things from God's divine perspective, it touches every aspect of our lives.

Often our spiritual vision is blinded by the glare of what our physical eyes see. I want to convince you that it is more important to make sure your spiritual eyes can see clearer than almost anything else that you do. If you can embrace this spiritual truth, then half of your battle has been fought and won.

## "Is your spiritual vision blinded?"

Psalms 119:18 teaches that there are wonderful things in God's law, which is the Word of God, the Bible. Through reading the Bible, we learn how God wants us to live. And God's teaching through his word changes lives profoundly. When we say to God "open our eyes," we're asking for his supernatural help. If God does not open our eyes, we will not see the wonderful things of his Word. We are helpless within ourselves to see spiritual wonderment. Ask God for supernatural illumination when praying and reading his word. To see the beauty, the glory, and all God's wonderment, we must ask God to—*open our eyes*! In the hymn, "Open My Eyes, That I May See," the writer says:

> Open my eyes that I may see,
> Glimpses of truth Thou hast for me;
> Place in my hands the wonderful key,
> That shall unclasp and set me free.
> Silently, now I wait for Thee,
> Ready my God, Thy will to see;
> Open my eyes, illumine me, Spirit divine." [13]

Spiritual eyes are eyes that hope in Christ. The fight to see spiritually is a fight to believe, have faith, and trust in God. Do your spiritual eyes have 20/20 vision? Can you see him molding, perfecting and implementing his will for your life? Don't you see him standing with outstretched arms waiting to commune with you?

The very first time that I was told to use my spiritual eyes came as a true revelation. This was after my corneal transplant surgeries, although I could see my vision was still challenged. I didn't have RGPs, and I had misplaced my eyeglasses while visiting my sister in Atlanta. At the time, she was going through breast cancer, and we were in a rush to leave for her doctor's appointment. I left the house, asking God to give me strength to be a support to her and strength for the visual limitations that I would face until I could find my eyeglasses.

When we got into the car a voice on the radio said, "God wants you to use your spiritual eyes today." My sister turned and inquired if I heard what the lady had just said. The voice on the radio said it again. "God wants you to use your spiritual eyes today." My brother-in-law, sister, and I shouted praises to God. We agreed that God was confirming that he was with us. Before we could finish praising, the voice on the radio said, "God is using you so that his glory can be revealed." Again, the voice on the radio repeated the statement. Now, this was truly a word from God. That statement ministered to my sister's breast cancer and all the concerns and prayers that we had lifted up to God pertaining to her challenge.

Without any doubts, we knew that God had just spoken through the radio. We were like the three Hebrew boys in the fiery furnace when the king asked, "Didn't we throw three men into the fire? I see four men walking around in the flames and one of them looks like an angel" (Daniel 3:25). In the natural eye, you saw only three people sitting in the car. But using our spiritual ears and eyes, there was a fourth person, a spiritual being, in the car with us on that day.

We were not the same. We were transformed into empowered ambassadors, filled with God's grace and mercy. No longer were we afraid of cancer, KC, and anything else that we would have to go through on that day. Whose report were we going to believe? We were going to believe the report of the Lord and his report said healed and victory!

In our daily activities, the Holy Spirit uses God's words through scriptures, fellowship, and devotional practices to develop our spiritual eyes. Ephesians 1:18 says, "The eyes of your understanding being enlightened; that ye may know what is the hope of his calling, and what the riches of the glory of his inheritance in the saints." Truly, when the eyes of our understanding are enlightened, we have deeper insight and know with confidence what hope is and how glorious the riches of his inheritance are upon those who believe.

God has freed us to break out of our limits and boxes by using our spiritual eyes. We see God when we observe him. When we consciously observe him, we create a world in which holy things can be observed. When we do not put our attention on him, we do not see the effects of his existence.

In order for me to write this book, my spiritual eyes were open. God wanted me to tell the world that he designed us to commune with him and him with us. If we ever hope to walk through this world victoriously with the circumstances around us, we must learn to see God not only in the heavenly realm, but also in our everyday experiences. The range of our vision must be enlarged to perceive his purposes. Once we've invited God to open our spiritual eyes, we will enjoy the benefits of seeing and knowing the depths of his great love.

While searching the scriptures, I wanted to know what the Word had to say about eyes, eyesight, and vision. To my delight, I came across many scriptures and teachings. Mark 8:18 asks a very thought-provoking question: "Do you have eyes but fail to see, and ears but fail to hear? And don't you remember?" Then Matthew 13:16 says, "Blessed are your eyes for they see and your ears for they hear."

I began to meditate on the scriptures and teachings that I had read. I asked the Holy Spirit to give me an understanding. After a few minutes, the light bulb of interpretation was switched on. I began to understand that if we are going to walk a walk that is worthy and pleasing to the Lord, then our eyes, ears, minds, and hearts must be open and alert to God's working in our lives. God wants us to come out of the "fog" of life's problems, circumstances, and situations that keep us in bondage and darkness. He's given us a way of escape out of all things. It is only when we seek him that we will see and understand the divine purpose that brings life, light, and liberation.

I've come to the full knowledge that my passion and purpose is to help others see God by having 20/20 spiritual vision. Christians and non-Christians come to God and don't really know what to do with him. We appreciate him in his sovereignty but fail to realize just how close we are to him as spiritual beings living as human beings.

I pray that this chapter will create a desire in you to know God, draw closer to him, and that you will open your spiritual eyes and see him work in your life like never before. With new conviction, we can all sing, "Amazing grace, how sweet the sound, that saved a wretch like me. I once was lost but now I'm found, was blind but now I see."

# Are Angels Watching Over You?

"Ask your angels to stay as near to you as they can;
to help keep your vision clear and your presence simple,
so in all the days to come there will be
a radiance and Glory in your spirit."
- Karen Goldman - [14]

Do you believe that there are angelic beings in the atmosphere? Do you believe that there are angels watching over you? Well, I do. I've learned to call on my angels as the above quote indicates.

If God created angels and he created man, doesn't it seem reasonable that he would have his heavenly beings watching over his earthly beings? I'm sure you can come up with more than one occasion when a divine intervention took place in your life. Think about it.

You're probably asking, "How do angels apply to my situation or circumstance?" By now, you should have gathered that my whole base for writing this book, teaching its principles, and living victoriously is from a spiritual dimension. "God is a Spirit and they that worship him must worship him in spirit and in truth" (John 4:24). Just as I believe that God is a Spirit, I also believe that angels are spiritual beings created by God to serve him and are sent by God to watch over the human race, to deliver his message, to guard and protect us from danger, and to do battle on our behalf.

In order to appreciate my belief in angels, I'll have to take you back to when I was sixteen years old. A rumor had circulated that there would be a fight in the school's cafeteria. I had no idea that I was the intended victim. When I began to eat my lunch, a milk carton was thrown, and it landed in my tray. A young lady began calling me out by name. A fear came over me that I had never felt in my entire life. With my head bowed, I prayed, "Lord, if I ever needed you, I sure do need you right now."

Suddenly, three things happened to me. First, when I raised my head from that plea for help, I wasn't afraid anymore. My hands had stopped shaking. Second, I felt a powerful, glowing presence encircling me. It felt as though angels had lifted their wings and formed a shield of protection around me. Third, a quiet inner voice deep within said, "You are not alone—go forth!"

As I walked toward my angry classmate, an inner voice told me what to say and do. I whispered in her ear, "Have I ever done anything to hurt you?" She didn't answer. I took the milk carton and placed it into her hands. I told her that I was going back to my seat, and that if she really wanted to hit me, then she should aim straight. I turned my back and walked away. I could feel the shield of protection moving with me. She didn't throw the milk carton, but instead she turned around and walked away.

There was no fight that day. The crowd in the cafeteria couldn't understand what had just happened. I knew what happened. God dispatched guardian angels to protect me from danger and to do battle on my behalf. Ever since that day, I've called on God for help, and he's never left me alone.

---

"Have you experienced a divine intervention?"

---

During my period of being functionally blind, guardian angels watched over me day and night.

About two years before my first corneal transplant, I was in an automobile accident. Out of nowhere, I was side-struck by another vehicle coming out of an apartment complex. The impact was so hard it sent my minivan into a spin and my eyeglasses were knocked off my face. I wasn't wearing a seat belt, and I was partially knocked out of the driver's seat.

I was holding onto the steering wheel while trying to focus and get back into the correct lane. The minivan was speeding forward into oncoming traffic. It went ramming down the sidewalk, knocked over a telephone pole, and speeded back into oncoming traffic. In my twisted position, my foot couldn't reach the break. I just knew my life had ended and in the next few seconds there was going to be a fatal crash and I was about to go to my heavenly home to meet my maker.

Instantly, a powerful force shield took control of the car and turned everything around. I found myself sitting on the seat in an upright position. My minivan was back in the correct lane and had come to a complete stop. Just like that, the madness stopped and for a few seconds the world stood still. Without a doubt, I knew my guardian angels were on duty.

People began rushing to the minivan. The young lady whose car had broadsided my minivan rushed over to see if I was living or dead. Immediately, she recognized me. We had grown up in the same church. I was ready to get out of the car, but somebody kept telling me to stay in until the police came. I got out of the minivan, stood next to it, and looked at the devastation.

The passenger's side was bent in from the front of the minivan to the back. My side of the automobile was picture-perfect with not one scratch. By this time, the young lady was sobbing and hugging me. She kept saying over and over to me, "Brenda, you could have been killed. Angels were watching over you."

Yes, indeed angels were watching over me. When I think back over that situation, I get chills remembering how I felt when my eyeglasses came off my eyes and things went fuzzy wuzzy. Maybe, it was a good thing I couldn't see clearly. The shock of seeing it all could have taken me out with heart failure. Nevertheless, I was functionally blind and couldn't see, but my guardian angels stepped in and took control.

Another angelic encounter came in yet another car accident. After my first corneal transplant, I had healed well enough to wear a rigid gas permeable contact lens again. I was in the driver's seat, and the impact of the collision caused the air bag to explode in my face. The air bag shielded the broken windshield glass from my face. When the firemen were removing me from the twisted minivan, they observed that I was bleeding from my right eye.

I was conscience but very shaken up. Surprisingly, I was able to inform them that I was wearing a hard contact lens. The fireman couldn't locate the lens in the right eye. I was afraid that my new corneal graft was in danger and all the effort of waiting and receiving a transplant had been wasted.

I could feel the presence of a circular shield all around me. I remembered thinking to myself that I had experienced this familiar presence before. Even I was amazed at how well I was functioning in the midst of the wreckage around me. *Lord, please save my eye*, was my silent prayer.

Quietly, the small inner voice of the Holy Spirit spoke to me and said, *Your eyes are fine … I'm with you.*

There was no damage to my eyes in any way. Again, guardian angels were with me. Although I acquired cuts from broken glass, facial bruises, skin burns from the air bag, and a dislocated big toe, my life and my eyes were spared.

A few weeks after the accident, while grocery shopping, an older gentleman approached me and remarked kindly, "What happened to you? It looks like everybody had a stick in the fight except you." I was really glad that he asked because it gave me an opportunity to give witness to how God sends divine intervention. By the time I finished telling him about guardian angels and how God saved me and my eyes, he was praising God with me.

There have been other divine interventions throughout my life; these are only three experiences that confirmed to me the existence of angels. I believe that God has given us everything that we need on this earth to stay divinely connected to him. When we learn to call on these resources, we invite God in to orchestrate a divine presence and authority to operate on our behalf.

I pray that this chapter will cause you to believe and call upon God's angels. Know that his angels are with you and ready and willing to help you with whatever will bring you peace. Learn to call on your guardian angels and ask them to surround you with an extra insulation of protective love. Ask them to help you throughout the day to have divine interventions, glorious and wonderful experiences, and to feel the peace of God within your heart, mind, body, and soul.

# Do You Know Him?

"Jesus Christ is God's everything for man's total need."
- Richard Halverson - [15]

Do you have someone who has made a great impact on your life? Outside of your immediate family members, name two of them. Think about it.

My two most important people are Jesus Christ and my eye doctor! There are other people that have been a great influence in my life and to which I am extremely grateful. I am thankful that I had Christian parents that introduced Jesus in my life at a young age. Along with this introduction came the instructions, "seek him for yourself and develop your own personal relationship with the Lord." Now, as for my eye doctor, living with KC leaves you no alternative. You must have an eye care professional to even hope to have some degree of functional vision.

In this chapter, I will talk about these two men. First, I will invite you to develop a relationship with the greatest man whom has ever walked this earth, Jesus Christ. It is a personal relationship with God through faith in Jesus. Just mentioning Jesus' name has been likened unto an ointment that nourishes, illuminates, and stills an anguished soul. God wants to come and live in your heart and have daily fellowship with you.

Secondly, I'll introduce you to Dr. Scott McGregor, whom I believe, is one of God's appointed earth angels, specializing in restoring sight through the fitting of specialty contact lenses. Finding a KC physician and contact lens fitter is not an easy task. I recommend anyone who needs a contact lens fitter because of KC or any other cornea disorders to make an appointment with Dr. Scott McGregor and let him become your eye care professional.

• • • • •

### Getting to Know Jesus Christ

When you want to know someone, you spend time with him or her, right? You spend time conversing with them, sharing your feelings, thoughts and hopes, and listening to one another. When one person loves another, they want to be with the person whom they love because love seeks to be with the object of its love. It is the same way with Jesus. You have to make an effort just as you would in your interaction with others. He promised that he would never leave us alone. He is standing and waiting with outstretched arms to whom ever wants to make him Lord of their lives.

So I ask, "Do you know Jesus? Or do you just know about Jesus?" Knowing about someone is not the same thing as knowing them. I believe just about everybody knows who Jesus is. They know that he was born in a manger. They know about the things that he did while he was on earth.

And, they know about how he died on a cross. They know a lot about Jesus, but they don't know Jesus.

Bebe Winans, Kurt Carr, Hezekiah Walker, and many others have put to song and music the question, "Do You Know Him?" All over the world, preachers, teachers, evangelists, missionaries, and various forums proclaim God's existence. No one will have the excuse of telling God that they never heard of Jesus Christ, which is his gift of salvation to humankind. God has made sure that we heard because he has put the knowledge out here for us to make a choice.

How do we get to know him? The Bible says that when we can say, "Jesus is Lord," and believe in our hearts that he died and was raised from the dead to save us, and then we can say that we really know him. "That if thou shalt confess with thy mouth the Lord Jesus, and shalt believe in thine heart that God hath raised him from the dead, thou shalt be saved. For with the heart man believeth unto righteousness; and with the mouth confession is made unto salvation (Romans 10:9–10)."

In order to grow and have an intimate and life changing relationship with Jesus Christ you must invest time in getting to know him. The more time you invest the deeper and more fulfilling the relationship becomes. It is a lifelong commitment to keep getting to know Jesus better. We get to know him through communicating with him in prayer, talking to him, listening for his "still small voice", and growing in our understanding of him through his word, the Bible.

Do you really know him in a personal way? Does his Spirit live in your heart and guide you? He wants you to know him as your personal Lord and Savior. You can know him if you will invite him to come and live within your heart. Getting to know Jesus and making him the center of your life will determine not only your values and lifestyle, but your eternal destiny as well. "For whosoever shall call upon the name of the Lord shall be saved (Romans 10:13)."

The real question now becomes, "What do you choose to do with him?" Will you accept or reject him? That knowledge is in your heart because God has put it there. You may choose to ignore it and refuse to accept Jesus Christ. On the other hand, you may choose to believe in him, receive him, and become a child of God. "But as many as received him, to them gave he power to become the sons of God, even to them that believe on his name (John 1:12)."

Is God knocking on your heart? Is he trying to gain access? If God has asked to come into your heart and life, then there is no middle ground. Making no decision to accept him is the same as rejecting him. If you do not say yes, you have therefore said no. Jesus said, "He that is not with me is against me: and he that gathereth not with me scattereth (Luke 11:23)."

The way of keeping an ongoing relationship with Jesus Christ is to keep believing and receiving what he has done for you. Things will start to change in your life and old habits will begin to be shaped by your new life in Christ. Begin sharing with others that you are now a child of God. Find and join a church home where Christians meet together, encourage and support each other, as well as grow together. "Therefore if any man be in Christ, he is a new creature: old things are passed away; behold, all things are become new (II Corinthians 5:17)."

Invite Jesus as your Lord and Savior right now by bowing your head and saying this simple prayer.

"Lord Jesus, I am a sinner and I ask for your forgiveness. I believe that you died for my sins

and that you rose from the dead. Lord, thank
you for saving me. Come into my heart and life.
Help me to live each day for you. In Jesus' name,
Amen."

God's word has assured us that when you invite Jesus into
your heart and life, you become a part of God's family and
your name is written in the lamb's book of life. God keeps
his word. "And this is the record that God hath given to us
eternal life, and this life is in his Son. He that hath the Son
hath life; and he that hath not the Son of God hath not life.
These things have I written unto you that believe on the
name of the Son of God; that ye may know that ye have
eternal life, and that ye may believe on the name of the Son
of God. 1 John 5:11–13)."

"Is Jesus Christ your everything?"

• • • • •

## Getting to Know Dr. Scott McGregor

"It's not about the destination but the discoveries you make
along the way," said the voice coming from the television. It
was amazing how those words jumped into my spirit at that
exact moment.

It was Monday, April 14, 2008. I was in Dallas, Texas,
and just arising from an afternoon nap. My husband and I
had spent the earlier part of the day with my newly found
eye care professional. As you read in the Foreword, Dr.
Scott McGregor is the inventor of the Mac-G Lenses.

These specialty-designed lenses revolutionize contact lens fitting and wear for those who are difficult or impossible to fit. This new technology combines comfort and vision as never before in gas permeable lenses. Dr. McGregor and I share a similar mission, which connects the passion of our pain—to help others experience clear vision and to live a purposed-filled life.

In 1984, when first diagnosed with KC, I knew that this eye disease was going to take me on a journey whether I wanted to go or not, and the final destination is yet to be known. Its course would lead me to meet many people and make interesting discoveries along the way. Amazingly, at the height of these discoveries would be my reason for driving seven hours to see an eye doctor. Dr. McGregor offers advice to KC patients via the National Keratoconus Foundation's message board link. At the gentle urging of the Holy Spirit, I was led to visit his Web site and to send him an e-mail. Within one week, our e-mails turned into a scheduled appointment. By divine design, fate and destiny connected us because this angel and workman of God could resurrect my sight.

It did not take long to realize that I was in the company of a compassionate physician that had dealt with the tedious and time consuming process of contact lens fitting for a KC patient.

"I've been waiting on your appointment for the past three weeks." He smiled warmly. "I couldn't rest well knowing that with bilateral transplants you were seeing 20/40 and 20/50 with visual aids when you could be seeing 20/20 in contact lenses that provide both comfort and better vision."

It was a change to know that an eye care professional was excited to take my case rather than being overwhelmed due to the complexities of finding the perfect fit for my astigmatic KC eyes.

"She's a veteran, but be gentle with her," his words guided his capable assistant while he dabbed at my teary eyes with a Kleenex tissue. "It's frightening and painful having something invade your eyes. Her eyes have been poked at for years."

"Yes, they have," I confirmed while choking back a sob. However, deep in my spirit, I was shouting with joy, and I wanted to scream out, *but this time it's going to be worth it!*

During the examination, while changing from one lens to another, my tearing was quite evident. It took self-control to hold myself together and to keep from sobbing tears of joy. I wanted to tell Dr. McGregor how I had prayed for a doctor who had empathy for patients like me. I wanted to tell him of the times that I sat outside in my car, dreading an eye appointment with my contact lens fitter. I wanted to tell him about the many times I had cried and the tears that I hold back from doctors who don't seem to care about me or the quality of sight I experience. I wanted to tell him how lonely, isolated, and devastated I often feel because of my poor vision. For some reason, I wanted to tell him everything because I sensed he had a tremendous capacity of heart and could truly understand.

Instead, I wiped my tears, pulled myself together, and smiled. All the while, I silently gave thanks to God for his angel and workman that was here on earth and now taking care of my eyes. Later, I learned of Dr. McGregor's awesome testimony, which he speaks of in the foreword of this book. Once again, destiny and divine design comforts my soul.

Two days later, when it was time to say good-bye, I left with my new Mac-G Lenses, seeing 20/20, and could read four out of six letters on the 20/15 row. I was beyond overjoyed! The first mind-blowing fact was that the lenses were made locally and came back the same day of the first fitting. Normally, it takes three to four weeks for KC prescriptions, and they can be sent as far away as Australia. The second mind-blowing fact is that you don't know you have the Mac-G Lenses on. It's amazing how a rigid gas permeable lens can feel like velvet cotton in your eyes. The Mac-G Lens is simply phenomenal.

I didn't want to say good-bye to Dr. McGregor and his staff when it was time to leave. Our new doctor-patient relationship seemed too brief. Easily, the professional handshake of doctor and patient turned into a heartfelt hug of celebration and thanksgiving. I was comforted in leaving knowing that God's purpose and plan would be fulfilled through our individual and joint efforts in helping others on their vision-challenged journeys. Indeed, I would see God's workman again on this KC journey because our work had only just begun.

I am confident that God has opened the secrets of his creation so that doctors may use them to heal the people that he created and loves. I am certain that Dr. McGregor's compassion and empathy for his patients lie within his own story of healing and restoration. His personal tragedy has shaped him and rewarded him with divine purpose as a giving and spirit filled physician. I realize that not every doctor-patient match is made in heaven but with Dr. Scott McGregor, I exclaim to the world that to know him and be under his professional care is definitely therapeutic and beneficial to my sight. Truly, with his handiwork as God's workman, I say without hesitancy, "I once was blind but now I see!"

Consider yourself blessed if you live in the Plano/Dallas, Texas regions because of your easy access to this physician. As for me and other KCer's who seek out his professional services and expertise, we will no doubt continue to make our pilgrimage to his place of service. Please visit his website at www.drscottmcgregor.com.

# The Beauty of KC

"One does not see anything until
one sees its beauty."
- Oscar Wilde—[16]

While spring-cleaning, I found a newsletter that is published by The National Keratoconus Foundation (NKCF). I've been receiving them for a while but just never took the time to fully read one. My eyes misted with tears when I read the stories about others all over the world that live daily with the challenges of KC.

Joy filled my spirit when I went online to www.nkcf.org and began to read about this disease. I practically shouted out of my chair when I clicked on the link http://kcvision.org that showed pictures of how the world appears to a KC patient. A picture is worth a thousand words, and finally, my family and friends could get a glimpse into my fuzzy wuzzy world. There were links for research, seminars, conferences, and many other resources that dealt with KC.

It was just too good to be true. I had found a society of people who could relate and understand the difficulties of doing simple everyday tasks because of unclear vision. I began my search for information about KC on the Internet, and I was not disappointed.

I found other KCers who had paved the way with information about KC and were opened to receiving e-mail and communicating with other KCers. For a minute, I thought I would be in information overload, but that was far from the truth. There can never be too much information found about KC. There needs to be more documented cases and case studies available.

I closed my eyes and allowed the Holy Spirit to speak. Deep down within, I heard that still quiet inner voice saying, "You're not alone. Write your testimony and put it in a book. There is a purpose for your affliction. Tell your story so that you may help others. Liken yourself as unto Paul on the Damascus Road. This is a thorn in your flesh, but my grace is sufficient unto you." Instantly, I received revelation and clarity of the purpose ahead of me.

Since my eyes of knowledge have been opened, I've taken an active role in educating people about KC and finding other KCers. I've contacted my local Organ and Tissue Donor organization and became a volunteer. Currently, I'm in the process of starting a KC support group in the Memphis area that is supported by the National Keratoconus Foundation. Also, I have written this book to add to other resource information to be available for anyone affected and interested in KC.

Is it possible there is a hidden beauty in the coned shaped spiral eyes of keratoconus patients? Many KCers have accepted KC as the way that God made us, and we move on with our lives. Many of us have seen a little something extra in having this condition. We've learned to cope and improvise. I believe KCers have a special place in their hearts for others with special needs. We've learned to reach out and to lend a hand so they don't have to go it alone.

---

"What is the hidden beauty in your challenge?"

---

Close your eyes and think of the things that your life challenges are teaching you. Open your mind and learn to your fullest capacity the facts about your diagnosis or situation. No matter what your challenges or obstacles may be in life, begin to see your future clearer than ever before. In the words of Bob Marley's song:

> I can see clearly now the rain has gone away,
> I can see all obstacles in my way.
> Gone are the dark clouds that had me blind.
> It's gonna be a bright sun-shiny day.
> Oh yes, I can make it now, the pain is gone,
> All of the bad feelings have disappeared.
> Here is the rainbow I've been praying for,
> It's gonna be a bright sun-shiny day. [17]

# KC Testimonials

The following pages are stories from KCers around the world who know fully the challenges of living with KC. I hope and pray that their testimonies will bear witness and bring healing to whatever challenges you may face.

*Name: Amanda*
*Age:* 39  *Location: Langley, British Columbia*

I was diagnosed with keratoconus in 2001. It was really difficult to wear rigid gas permeable lenses. However, my eye care technician was wonderful and advised me not to rely on glasses. So I suffered through the initial adjustments, and now it is not so bad. As a result of my diagnosis, I have a new outlook on my life and consider KC a blessing for a number of reasons. Here are just a few.

After ten years of going to school, I got my four-year degree in Child and Youth Care. Before KC, I never felt like I needed to rush. I obtained a B.A. all while still putting my two wonderful children first. They are now ages eleven and fourteen.

Before KC, we had never been on a family vacation. After learning that I had KC, we took a family vacation. We went to Westbank, British Columbia and had a great time. Since then we have been on lots of vacations, including Disneyland twice.

KC motivated me to get into the best physical shape that I've ever been in my life. In the last fifteen years, I've only ridden my bike about three times, but recently I biked twenty kilometers and loved it.

My husband lost some money in a business deal, and I realize it's small stuff now. I also spend a lot of money on dance for my girls and tap dance lessons for me, and it is worth every penny! Funny thing is, I am spending money on vacations and costumes, and I don't feel broke like I used to when I did not spend the money.

I've learned that although KC can be degenerative, it is not fatal. I know that if I were to leave this planet today, I would have no regrets because having KC has truly blessed my life.

*Name: LaShanna*
*Age:* 33  *Location: Mobile, Alabama*

I was first diagnosed with KC in 1998, in St. Louis, Missouri. I was treated with glasses, and I was told that the disease could progress at any time. My vision worsened in my right eye, and I was sent to a corneal specialist. They performed all the regular tests and suggested I get contacts. Now, that was not going to happen because I did not like water getting in my eyes. There was no way I was going to wear contacts. My doctor wrote another prescription for glasses and gave me my options. He advised that I would eventually need to get corneal transplants in both eyes and that my right eye was the worst.

In 1999, I got married and relocated to Mobile, Alabama. In 2000, my vision started to change again in both eyes. My diagnosis was that I needed a corneal transplant in my right eye. I was afraid, and I thought I was going to go blind. I did not want to have surgery, but it was my only option. I put it off for as long as I could and got another prescription for new glasses.

In 2001, I had my first corneal transplant. I was so afraid. I was in a new city, my family was in St. Louis, and this was really a tough time for me. Normally, during corneal transplant surgery, you are given a mild sedative and awake during the procedure. I was in such a state of anxiety until the surgeon put me to sleep with a general anesthesia. After the surgery, I just wanted to go home and sleep.

The next day was the worst day. After the medicines had worn off, my eye was puffy, swollen, and watery. I felt the stitches, and it was awful. Remember, this is the same person who doesn't like anything in her eyes—but eye drops and ointment became my two best friends. The stitches had to come out. The doctor could take them out once they healed or they would pop up to the surface themselves. Each time they came up to the surface, I experienced pain. It felt like a pin or knife sticking in your eye. Each time I had to endure the doctor putting tweezers in my eye to get it out. It happened so many times until I asked the doctor if I could have a pair of tweezers for the house. He just laughed, but he never gave me any.

My vision was not as bad as it was in the beginning, but I still had to wear glasses to correct my sight. I had to wait until my right eye was completely healed before my left eye was done. In 2002, my second transplant was completed. I was on my way to better sight, and then another obstacle came my way.

On November 16, 2003, I was involved in a car accident. I lost my sight completely in my healed right eye. I sustained a ruptured globe, detached retina, and an iris that was no longer there. The doctor said I would never see in my right eye again. I was devastated. My faith was tested but never broken. I almost went into a state of depression, but I knew I served a God who is able to turn all bad things around for the good. My left cornea graft is doing well. I still have some stitches in it, and I still wear glasses to correct my vision.

Living with KC is an adventure. The sun glare, the dry eyes, and not being able to drive at night because you can't see the words on street signs until you are on top of the sign. By that time, it is too late and you have to turn around to go back to where you came from. I pretty much only drive places where I know, especially at night. I have limited TV and computer usage time. My eyes start to dry out, and I have to rest them. My love for reading is hindered but not taken away. I used to read a book in a couple of days, but now I have to be mindful of my one eye and take it easy.

I joke around about only having one eye, but I promise I am okay with what God has destined for me. The main thing I want all the KCers to know is not to let this disease hinder you from doing whatever your heart desires. We may be limited, but we can do anything we put our minds to do. The best thing about this disease is my closer relationship with God. When you don't understand why things happen and you don't know what tomorrow holds, just know that he is the only one with the answers. I thank God each and every day for the life that he has given to me.

Therefore, I live my life victoriously!

## Name: Ian
### Age: 27 Location: Orlando, Florida

I was diagnosed with KC when I was twelve years old. At that time, my vision was poor but manageable. I spent a few years in glasses until the vision deteriorated to a point where glasses could no longer affect my vision positively. I spent several years in limbo. I was unable to be fitted for lenses and unable to see better than 20/200.

At that time, I entered into the visually impaired program at my high school. There I was taught many ways to deal with low vision. It was a difficult time, but after much searching my parents found a qualified lens fitter who was able to comfortably and properly fit me for Rigid Gas Permeable lenses.

Once I was fitted for lenses, my entire world changed. I was able to see 20/20. I still remember leaving the doctor's office and looking out the window of my parent's car to see the most beautiful thing ever: a discarded cigarette butt lying on the curb. It wasn't so much beautiful that someone had littered but it was amazing that I could actually see the cigarette. No wait! It was amazing that I could see the curb!

Later years, I had a transplant in my left eye. Initially, the results were unbelievable. I was able to see 20/40 with no correction of any kind. Over the following months, my vision declined to a level that was quite poor. I couldn't see the big E on the eye chart.

In 2008, I've had two subsequent surgeries to improve vision in the corneal-transplanted eye. Prior to this surgery, I had sixteen diopters of astigmatism. My doctors all claimed that it was the "hardest eye to fit/correct" in their years of practice. In any case, the miniARK, corneal wedge re-sectioning and relaxing incisions have left me with 1.5 diopters of astigmatism. And best uncorrected vision of 20/40 range. After three long years, a truly remarkable level of success was achieved from blind to sighted, back to blind, and finally sighted again; similar to pages from *Flowers for Algernon*. Through all of this, I've concluded that discouragement and frustration are easy to come by in this our shared burden of KC—but perseverance brings with it great rewards.

*Name: Safaa*
*Age: 34  Location: U.S.A.*

My story with KC begins as a ten-year-old girl living in Egypt. I was tall for my age, and I had to sit in the back of the class to avoid blocking the view of the blackboard from others. I started wearing glasses when I was sixteen but was never able to see well. At age eighteen, I was diagnosed with KC after visiting sixteen or more eye doctors. On one occasion, an optometrist prescribed a pair of glasses that made me feel like I was walking in a round tunnel when walking in a regular hallway. I can laugh about it now, but at the time, I felt so dizzy and uncomfortable.

Imagine a sand storm while wearing hard contact lenses and no sunglasses. I am sure you can only imagine the pain. I started wearing hard contact lens when I was twenty. In my country, we do not have labs that make specialty lenses so the doctor would try to find the best fit from a collection of lenses in his office. I experienced broken lenses, a lens lost through the sink drain, a lens stuck in the corner of my eye like a suction cup, lost under my eyelid, or popping out of my eye at anytime and anywhere. Finally, I had to use anesthetic drops in order to wear my lenses for two hours. During this time, I was almost a legally blind person.

The pair of lenses that I was wearing caused scaring to the eye tissue. If I had continued to wear them any longer, they would've done extreme damage. An optometrist in the United States explained that this pair of lens was sharp enough on my sensitive cornea that I could've used them for shaving instead. In spite of that, I have always been an A student and was blessed with a loving and caring family who offered me great support.

When I moved to the United States to do my graduate studies, I had to go to six doctors and try a variety of RGPs with no success. Then, by coincidence, a friend of a friend turned out to be an optometrist. This person has truly changed my life and was a blessing from God. He was very patient and understanding. It took us some time through trial and error to progress through custom-made RGPs that I could wear for a considerable number of hours. He always said that I picked the worst carrier for an eye condition because I am a bookworm and I spend long hours in front of the computer for work and research, which puts a lot of strain on my eyes.

Now, my optometrist has retired, and I have moved and need to find another eye doctor to help with my eyes. Finding another eye care professional to trust and feel at ease with is not easy based on my experience. Furthermore, I know there will be a day when I have to go through a transplant in my right eye, which is the one in worse condition, and I am trying my best to be emotionally and financially ready.

I've had my share of falling off the stairs because the steps were not quite in the place where I saw them. I've had my share of humiliation and embarrassment due to my vision problem. I've had my share of tears, headaches, eye ulcers, eyestrain, and pain. Sometimes, I couldn't even cry for fear that my contact lens would pop out of my eye. So, I had to postpone crying until I took off my contact lens.

I believe that everything happens for a reason, and we need to count our blessings instead of cursing our luck. When I see a blind person, I thank God for my KC even if it is my worst eye day. KC has surely changed my life. Knowing the problem is more than half the solution in our case. Having access to the KC message board and being able to share our experiences is wonderful. We can only live our lives once, so let's make the best out of it. Where there is a will, there is a way!

*Name: Doug*
*Age: 53  Location: Van Buren, Arkansas*

Reverend Doug Beasley started having trouble with his vision when he was five years old. In 1968, while in the eighth grade, he was diagnosed with keratoconus. He wore contact lenses for several years and was able to attain 20/20 vision. However, his vision slowly deteriorated. In 1980, due to a hydrops condition, he had no vision in his right eye. As a result, he could no longer wear his contact lens. His doctor placed him on the waiting list for a cornea transplant. In six weeks, a donor was found, and a transplant was performed successfully. One year after his first corneal transplant, Doug stated, "I could see the leaves on the trees. I could distinguish people's faces. I could see their freckles. I cried because I could see. I was blind, but now I see!" That quote became his motto, and he proudly wears it emblazoned across his tee shirt.

Keratoconus continued to advance in his left eye and two years later required transplant surgery. He waited six months for a donor the second time. However, the steroid he was given post-surgically may have caused premature cataracts. The cataracts were removed. One procedure was not successful. The new lens came out of its capsule, so the implant had to be redone. Now, Doug has 20/40 vision with glasses. The less than good news is that he had no binocular vision.

Since the cataract surgeries, his eye muscles were not aligned. Realignment requires several injections of oculinum (or Botox, a highly purified, stable form of Botulinum Toxin A that is used as an alternative to surgery to correct eye muscle misalignment.) Doug states that the injections are a nuisance because he can't drive immediately after a procedure. His last injection was in 1999.

Doug considers himself as a normal person and has never been depressed because of his vision difficulties. "Well, maybe the cataracts got me down a little," he confessed. "My vision fluctuates, so I need a new prescription every few months, and my insurance company won't cover it. There are some difficulties, but I deal with them. When I have trouble seeing, I move closer to the newspaper, chalkboard, or whatever. Keratoconus is an inconvenience and entails a lot of waiting. You see a lot of doctors, wait for your turn at a lot of clinics, wait for a cornea donation, wait for the transplant to heal, but seeing the leaves on the trees are worth the wait!"

Despite his vision difficulties over the years, Doug finished school, got a degree in music, did seminary work, married, and is now a music minister. He had to give up sports because he felt he couldn't protect himself from a ball that might hit him in the face, but he refused to feel sorry for himself and developed other interests. When volunteers were recruited to go to Honduras on a missionary trip, Doug signed on immediately. Grateful to the families who donated the corneas of their loved ones to him, he was eager to help other people with vision problems. "I went through a lot," Doug says. "Now I want to help others who are going through the same thing." The group took donated eyeglasses, and Doug helped with the eye tests. He found it humbling to help people who couldn't afford eye exams or spectacles. After his Honduras trip, Doug brought new enthusiasm to his work with ARORA, the Arkansas Regional Organ Recovery Agency. Each month, he puts up an ARORA display in the local Department of Motor Vehicles office and encourages people to sign the back of their driver's license, agreeing to be an organ donor. "I am living proof that corneal donation works. A friend of mine who had a heart transplant several years ago joins me. We make a great team."

In March 2003, Doug went to Mexico in a small, unmapped village and did eye exams and helped with a medical clinic.

In 2004, Doug was diagnosed as a Type II diabetic. His ophthalmologist states that there is no damage to his corneas due to the diabetes. Doug's cornea grafts are now twenty-six and twenty-eight years old and clear as a bell with no signs of rejection. His vision is 20/40 with a small prescription in his glasses.

In June 2005, Doug joined the Board of Directors for the Arkansas Lions Eye Bank and Laboratory and is a popular speaker for his Lion's Club district club meetings, as well as other eye support groups.

In March 2006, Doug began seeing flashes and fireballs in his left eye. He went to a Nero Ophthalmologist who sent him to a Retinal Specialist. The Retinal Specialist advised that there was nothing wrong with his eyes. Doug's vision remains 20/40, and he'll be keeping his annual visit to see his ophthalmologist.

In June 2006, Doug became president of the Van Buren Lion's Club and in 2007, Vice President of the Eye Bank Board. Ask him if he's healed, and I'm sure you'll get a heartfelt resounding *yes!* Visit Doug at http://www.vanburenlions.org.

*Name: Janet*
*Age:* 41 *Location: Chesapeake, Virginia*

I was diagnosed with KC in 2001. A routine visit to the eye doctor for new contacts revealed development of KC and the recommendation that I not wear contacts (which was not the best news for me). The ophthalmologist I was seeing told me that wearing contacts could possibly speed the progression of the disease. Over the next five years as my vision worsened, I visited two corneal specialists and several contact fitters with no positive results. Eventually, I refused to go for exams and only returned when my glasses broke.

My mother saw an episode on *Oprah* of medical miracles, which included a segment on the Boston Foundation for Sight. Dr. Perry Rosenthal developed the Boston Scleral Lens, which sits over the entire sclera (white portion) of the eye. These custom-made lenses contain fluid that fills in the irregular shape of the diseased cornea, therefore improving vision.

That was approximately three years into my journey with KC. I sent my records to Boston and was told at that point that I was not a good candidate. After two more years of struggling and with the looming possibility of failing the eye exam at the Department of Motor Vehicles to renew my license, it seemed as if the only option for me was to have a corneal transplant on both eyes.

In January of 2006, I read an article in *Good Housekeeping* about a woman with KC who had been to the Boston Foundation for Sight, and her vision had been restored. I was determined that I was *not* going to have my eyes cut on. Again, I contacted the Boston Foundation for Sight and was contacted by the staff and told that they thought they could help me. I was told that I needed to be prepared for a two-week stay in Boston and that the cost of the fitting and lenses was approximately $7,600.

I immediately thought of all the reasons that I couldn't possibly go to Boston for two weeks—what about my job, my kids, the expenses, et cetera? I was rejoicing because I was being accepted as a patient and scared to death that it would not happen. Within a week, the lines of communication through my church family were in full swing. Dinners and fundraisers were being organized by my family and friends. My parents offered to take care of my children, and all plans were falling into place. Now my biggest fear was that my friends and family would raise the funds to send me to Boston and it would be a failure.

On June 18, 2006, with my wonderful husband by my side, we flew to Boston for one of the most incredible experiences of my life. Meeting Dr. Perry Rosenthal was a life-changing experience for me. After struggling with the initial eye exam and answering questions, Dr. Rosenthal inserted several test lenses, and within minutes, I was reading the eye chart with one of my eyes.

I squealed with delight as I continued reading further and further down the eye chart as my husband watched in disbelief. Tears came to my eyes, and I was almost speechless as I looked next to me to see clearly the face of my hero. Dr. Rosenthal and his staff were incredible. We were given a tour of the facility and told that we were considered members of the family. Each morning we would check in with the office staff then make ourselves at home in the fully stocked kitchen area available to all patients. Also available for our use were TV, computer, and a lounging area. All the comforts of home were provided. I have never been involved with such a caring medical facility.

On our fifth day at the facility, we were in the kitchen/

conference room area waiting for one of my final exams. There was a man at the table wearing dark sunglasses, writing something in a notebook with his face almost directly on the paper. I immediately assumed that he was a patient and thought to myself how lucky I was to have my vision restored. We were called back to the examining room, and Dr. Rosenthal cleared me to return home.

He asked me if I would do something for him. For the man who had given me my life back, I would do anything! He told us that one of the large contributors for the Boston Foundation for Sight was at the facility, and he wanted me to share the story of how my family and friends had made it possible for my trip to Boston to become a reality. He escorted us back to the reception area, and there stood the man with the dark sunglasses that we had seen earlier in the conference room. Ten years earlier Dr. Rosenthal had restored his sight as well, and now he was one of the people that helped keep the foundation going.

Even though the lenses are expensive and it does require an extended stay in the Boston area, Dr. Rosenthal and his staff can help patients find free lodging with host families, and financial assistance is available. They will help with transportation if necessary and even offer meals for those long mornings and afternoons at the facility. They are the most incredible medical professionals I have ever been involved with, and I consider myself truly blessed that I was able to be a patient.

I returned to Chesapeake, Virginia, seeing clearly for the first time in many years. I was amazed at all I had been missing, including seeing the freckles on my children's faces and the new lines on my own! Life has been incredible since my trip to Boston. You don't realize how much you have been missing until you see it again. I hope that my story will benefit others and let them know about the amazing work that is being done in Boston.

Visit www.bostonsight.org for more detailed information and amazing stories of the many patients that have been helped at the Boston Foundation for Sight.

*Name: Colleen*
*Age:58   Location: Bottineau, North Dakota*

I am fifty-eight years old and have had KC for about thirty years. I was diagnosed at a medical center in North Dakota after getting very nearsighted very quickly. I started wearing contacts when I was thirteen, and my Optometrist always felt that had some relation to me getting KC. The old lenses in those days were not gas permeable, and being young, I wore them for extended periods of time.

We live in a very rural area of North Dakota. I flew to Portland, Oregon, and was fitted by Patrick Caroline, FAAO, in 2001. He was teaching at the School of Optometry, and now I see he presented at the 2007 Global Keratoconus Congress in Las Vegas. It is a small world of KC professionals that we deal with!

I have had only two fitters due to the insurance issue and where we live. I have lost contacts in swimming pools, in cars, at auditoriums while cheerleading before crowds, and numerous other places. The older I got and with the progression of the disease, I realized I could not afford to wait for a new lens and thus, took better care and fewer chances while swimming, skiing, snowmobiling, and other activities. I wish that I'd had all this wonderful information (found through the KC-Link Digest) about goggles years ago!

I've gone through numerous stages of progression, but for the past few years it seems to be slowing. I do not drive at night, and I have to "bank" my hours of wearing time. If I am going somewhere and need to see clearly, I make sure I have saved hours of wearing time for that event. I can get by with glasses but very poorly. I certainly need to stay around the house or very familiar surroundings when I am wearing glasses.

The famous "halo effects" are very evident for me. It

is very difficult to explain to people what we see and the nature of the disease. Some of the pictures submitted to the Web site have helped my husband see what I see. I wish we had more of these KC images. Dealing with a windy environment is very difficult, unless one wants to wear goggles at all times when outdoors.

I have earned a graduate degree in Communication Disorders and taught and practiced many years. I've learned to deal with this eye disease, but I do admit the older I get, the more it dictates what I feel I can and cannot do.

Thanks to the founders, doctors, and supporters of the National Keratoconus Foundation. A special thanks to Catherine Warren for helping so many of us through the NKCF Web site. The list of recommendations for different supplies that we need has truly been a blessing. I feel we all will see great advances in the research and treatment of KC in the years to come.

*Name: Angelo*
*Age:* 24 *Location: Melbourne, Victoria, Australia*

I was diagnosed with KC at eleven. Despite the severity of my condition, I never received any special treatment or reasonable adjustments. I attended a low-socioeconomic Catholic boy's school in the working class part of Melbourne. Together with my parents, they did not understand disability rights. My first visit with an ophthalmologist was around the age of fifteen; however, he declined to operate due to my age. I would eventually have my transplant at twenty years old.

Given the poor nature of my high school, none of my friends (a group of about thirty-five young men) got into university. University was simply an unrealistic option. The best prospect was to become a tradesman such as a plumber, electrician, carpenter, panel beater, etc. However, I really wanted to be a lawyer. My final year of high school was spent mostly in the public library with girls from the local catholic girl's school (I promise we did homework). I worked really hard and made it into law school—a Bachelor of Laws at Victoria University. I do not know why my ambitions were so different to those of my high school friends, but I suspect KC had something to do with it. I had a unique insight into life, which was unshared by others. I could see life clearly.

Law school was scary at first. My self-confidence was quite poor. Due to the high volume of reading in law, I had perceived KC as an insurmountable obstacle that would prevent me from performing well. I was so cynical that I had considered "dropping out" on a number of occasions. In my mind, and, in hindsight, wrongly so I might add, there was no way I could pass a law degree and get a graduate job as a KCer. That all changed when it was suggested I publish my work for contract law, a first year subject, in a law journal. I had never considered an undergraduate could publish. I now know this is quite an unusual achievement for an undergraduate reflecting on the fact that some full lecturers are yet to publish a fully refereed journal article.

I expanded my essay considerably and eventually published my work in the fully refereed section of the Bond Law Review—the only undergraduate to do so in the journal's eighteen-year history. Note also that this journal article was written while going through corneal eye transplant surgery and subsequent recovery in 2003–2004 at twenty years of age. My publication was also listed as research output for the university. Again, I am the only undergraduate at my law school to do so and even more so significant, an undergraduate with KC!

Despite KC and my background, I have now finally realized my dream of being a lawyer. In November 2007, I completed my Bachelor of Laws with First Class Honors as the Valedictorian of the Faculty of Business and Law and top graduating student among 1,301 graduates. Now, I am working as an Associate Lecturer-in-Laws and will commence work as a Judges' Associate from September 2008 for a period of twelve months. Having been accepted into the University of Oxford, I will pursue postgraduate studies in law in the United Kingdom after my Associateship (yes, I am still pinching myself!).

Aside from reaching my educational goals, getting fit has been another accomplishment. The transplant got me down, and I gained weight. Within fourteen months, I gained twenty-six kilograms of body weight (to get to 106 kilograms body weight) and lost strength to lifting fifty kilograms on the bench press. Now, one and a half years later, I have lost thirty-four kilograms (now at seventy-two kilograms body weight) and lift 102 kilograms on the bench press. I've bounced back, and now I'm in great shape. Exercise has helped me overcome a psychological barrier of KC.

Lastly, the only debilitating feature of KC is the unfortunate mistake of actually believing that it in fact debilitates. I would argue that KC in fact strengthens in resolve, in persistence, in ambition. It is indeed a unique gift that has enhanced my love for social justice, my passion for community, and my desire to help people in my career.

## Name: *Virginia*
## Age:56   Location: *Indiana*

The word *keratoconus* has always been a part of my family's vocabulary. My sister was diagnosed with KC when I was six years old and received her first contact lenses in 1958. I was nine when I began wearing glasses, but I never wore them much because they didn't seem to help. At age fourteen, the doctor began talking to me about contact lenses. I resisted, because I remembered the difficulties my sister experienced with her contacts. In 1966, I relented and got my first pair of hard contacts. To my amazement, I could see. I threw away my glasses! My KC didn't give much difficulty through my school years but definitely was an annoyance.

After my sweetheart and I married, we moved to the island of Bonaire, where we worked with a missionary radio station, broadcasting God's Word around the world. On Bonaire, I learned the value of spare contact lenses when traveling. I was standing in the beautiful, warm, clear Caribbean putting on my snorkeling mask when my lens popped out. The Caribbean didn't look quite the same after that. Fortunately, I had spare lenses. Later when we moved to South Africa, I made sure I was equipped with a spare pair of contacts and enough solutions to last for three years. I was able to occasionally find solutions in Johannesburg and Durban, but I was never able to find an ophthalmologist or contact lens fitter for my KC eyes.

After about three years in South Africa, we moved to Swaziland, Africa. There were no KC eye doctors there either. My eyes did fairly well during our eighteen years in Africa. I did manage to get my eyes examined every three years when we were back in the U.S., and I needed new lenses every time. Sometimes my eyes would begin to give me trouble before the three years was over. I thought it seemed to be associated with pregnancy.

My sister continued to have difficulties with her eyes. In 1978, she had corneal transplant surgery. Unknown to the doctors, the man who donated the cornea had died from rabies. My sister had begun to see with her transplanted eye better than she had for a long time. Within weeks, she began to have horrible headaches. She had contracted rabies from the donor. After a short, agonizing illness, God took her home. She left four young children and a husband who loved her.

In 1989, we finally returned to America to stay. My eyes continued to worsen. I wore glasses over my contacts to help with the astigmatism, and of course, my age made reading glasses inevitable. I was a little apprehensive about a transplant. I knew that what happened to my sister was the exception, but it did bring home the dangers involved in any surgery. In August 2004, I received my new cornea. I was a little disappointed with the immediate results, but it was better than it had been. The pain I had been suffering for months was gone. I could read stop signs. After fourteen months, the stitches were taken out. There was not much change in my vision, but receiving new glasses helped some. I was then scheduled to have relaxing incisions and cataract surgery. These surgeries improved my vision dramatically.

My eyelid had begun to droop badly after all the surgeries and was impairing my vision. I had eyelid surgery, which also was an improvement. My vision is now 20/30 in that eye. It is better than my left eye with its contact lens. I still need glasses to help with the astigmatism and with reading. I've had rejection problems, and I'm using Prednisone drops once a day for the rest of my life. I also have problems with dry eye and have to use drops, keep a humidifier running, and take supplements for dry eye.

My day and night vision is greatly improved, but I still don't drive much after dark. I can read for pleasure and sew again. KC is still a nuisance but not really life altering for me. I use larger print on the computer and make adjustments where needed. I am now able to read street signs without stopping the car and walking back to read the signs. Things still look a little fuzzy but are so much better. I do make odd mistakes in reading when I can't tell for sure what the letters are. But it is so much better.

I am thankful for the excellent doctors God put in my way to care for my eyes. I believe that I could not have had better. I am also thankful for the family who allowed the corneas of their loved one to be used to give someone else sight. It was a very humbling experience to think that because someone died, I can see. Words do not come that would adequately express my thanks to that family, but I do thank them from the bottom of my heart.

As I think of my life with KC, I am reminded of a young girl at the school where I work. She completely lost her sight in high school. She learned how to make her way through the halls and graduated with very good grades. What really impressed me was that she was a cross-country runner. She did not let blindness rob her of the joy of running. She found a helper to run with her. She held on to her helper's elbow to run and never did come in last. She is an example of trust and making the best of something that would make lesser people give up and/or become depressed.

One of my favorite poems was penned by Fannie Crosby (blind since infancy). She emphatically shares speaks of happiness and contentment although she could not see. It is my hope and prayer that KCers around the world will take this poem to heart. Read her poem and I pray it will minister to you as it has to me through the years. You can find the poem online at www.wikipedia.org by searching for Fannie Crosby.

*Name: Dimitry*
*Age 30 Location: Israel*

My dream of becoming an astronaut seems more distant than ever since I've been diagnosed with KC. I used to have very good eyesight. I only wore glasses once, for a school play, and they didn't have lenses. Even in college, when my eyesight started to decline, I could sit in the last row of the largest lecture hall and experience no discomfort or difficulty reading the board. My symptoms first became noticeable about six months after college, when I began working as a programmer. At first, it was just a mild blurring and light sensitivity, which I attributed to fatigue and eyestrain. When it started to progress (on the left eye) and the dry air from the a/c started to cause burning sensations, I turned to doctors.

It was October 2005, and for the following year, I saw six ophthalmologists, a neurologist, a bunch of optometrists, and went through a battery of various fits and tests, including MRI. The results were basically the same. "You have normal astigmatism, that's all. You had it since birth, but somehow didn't notice it or that it might have progressed. All you need is glasses. What do you mean nobody can fit you with glasses? Well, I can't help you, but here is yet another test for you, maybe it will show something." The last doctor even suggested that all these symptoms were only in my imagination.

Double vision became evident sometimes in May 2006, after which there was a three-month-long sudden burst of progression, affecting mostly the previously unaffected right eye. At this time, I turned to the so-called "alternative medicine" (shameful but true). To my defense, I didn't really know it was alternative. It was called "meditative eye exercises" (spawned from yoga, most likely), and mega-vitamins (a naturopathic practice). Fortunately, I knew enough not to try the second one as instructed—vitamin overdose can be just as dangerous as vitamin deficiency. I did try the regular doses of vitamins. Neither had any noticeable effect, but after a few months the progression did slow down. But, as I know now, short periods of sudden progression are perfectly natural with KC.

Ironically, the progression came to a halt only after I dropped both vitamins and exercises, not that there was any causal relation in the first place. In fact, I soon learned exactly how useless eye exercises and vitamin supplements really are, but that's another story. People in such vulnerable states of despair might try anything, no matter the cost, so I was fortunate not to come across any other "alternative cure-all" during this period. A full session with a Philippine healer, for example, might have cost me my entire savings, while yielding no results.

Afterwards, I returned to the real medicine, but this time turned to online medical sources first. After spending hundreds of hours at it, I learned a lot, including such weird terms like "monocular diplopia" and "bilateral polyopia." It's incredible how much you can learn simply by entering "double vision" in Google and then going from there. I found about twenty conditions that could cause symptoms similar to mine. Most were already ruled out by all the tests, leaving only astigmatism, dry eye, and keratoconus.

This is how I first heard about the latter. Online I began to learn about the tests needed to diagnose KC. It seemed like a corneal topography was the most sensible next step. Thusly armed, I visited the eighth doctor on my quest for diagnosis and stated from the start that I didn't want to hear about glasses, I've already done all the standard tests, I've never had clinical astigmatism before, and I had "severe monocular diplopia with rapid progression periods."

I'm not sure why, maybe I did say something right this time and it clicked, or maybe it was simply the only option left, but she suggested corneal topography even before I managed to ask for it. She knew of only one doctor with a topographer. It took him only forty seconds to diagnose KC. He didn't specialize in it, so I was referred to the one who did, my current doctor. He confirmed the diagnosis (he has a topographer in his office) and fitted me with RGPs in two hours. Ironically, his clinic was basically around the corner from my house, and he was covered by my insurance, so I could've visited him first and been spared a year and a half of trouble and suffering. It's a very good example of how difficult it is to exhaust conventional options. Even if half a dozen doctors can't help you, it doesn't mean that you're beyond help in terms of the conventional medicine—far from it.

The diagnosis was made in January 2007, three weeks after I quit my job because I couldn't work anymore, not knowing what's happening to me and being forced to squint nine hours a day. Now, consider the possibility that instead of playing with yoga and vitamins for three months, I could push the conventional approach further and be diagnosed earlier. I could've kept my job. I'm lucky, because I was going to quit anyway, eventually. But what if I wasn't? The job was actually a very good one—for some of my friends it would've been a dream come true (their words, more or less).

After a month of wearing contact lenses, I was able to score 20/20 (corrected) on the eye chart, back from as low as 20/80 just prior to diagnosis. Life goes on. In fact, I now know so much about eyesight, I sometimes pass for an eye doctor. I even used my newly acquired free time to learn more about alternative medicine, so that I won't be duped again. And it turned out that I have been duped a lot by it my whole life. But that's another story.

# Donating Eye Tissue

"Don't think of organ donations as giving up part of
your self to keep a total stranger alive. It's really a total
stranger giving up almost all of themselves to keep
part of you alive."
-Author Unknown- [18]

Oftentimes, I refer to the Apostle Paul's statement in 1
Corinthians 12:1, "Now concerning...I would not have
you ignorant." Surely, I will not have you ignorant or not
being aware of the importance and benefits of organ/tissue
donations.

In my online research and quest for answers, I discovered the Eye Bank Association of America's Web site. In
being a recipient of two corneas, I too, like thousands of
others, acknowledge donors and the families of loved ones
who give the gift of sight. From this Web site, my eyes and
awareness were open and I left with a better understanding
of eye tissue donations.

A few of the frequently asked questions about eye/tis-
sue donations are as follows. I encourage you to visit the

Eye Bank Association of America's Web site and learn more about its services and organization. Visit their link at www. restoresight.org.

*What is the cornea?* The cornea is the clear tissue covering the front of the eye. It is the main focusing element of the eye. Vision will be dramatically reduced if the cornea becomes cloudy from disease, injury, or infection.

*What is corneal blindness?* Corneal blindness is a disorder that results from the cornea becoming clouded, making a person blind. This condition can result from a variety of diseases, injury, or infection.

*What is a corneal transplant?* This is a surgical procedure that replaces a disc-shaped segment of an impaired cornea with a similarly shaped piece of a healthy donor cornea.

*Is the whole eye transplanted?* No. Only the cornea can be transplanted. The entire eye may be used for research and education.

*How prevalent is corneal transplantation?* Corneal transplant is one of the most frequently performed human transplant procedures. Since 1961, more than 549,889 corneal transplants have been performed, restoring sight to men, women, and children ranging in age from nine days to 103 years.

*How successful is corneal transplantation?* Over ninety percent of all corneal transplant operations successfully restore the corneal recipient's vision.

*Why should eyes be donated?* There is no substitute for human tissue. The transplantation process depends upon the priceless gift of corneal donation from one human to the next. Donated human eyes and corneal tissue are used for research, education, and transplantation.

*Who can be a donor?* Anyone can. Cataracts, poor eyesight, or age do not prevent you from being a donor. It is important for individuals wanting to be donors to inform family members of their wishes.

*Will the quality of medical treatment be affected if one is a known donor?* No. Strict laws are in existence, which protects the potential donor. Legal guidelines must be followed before death can be certified. The physician certifying a patient's death is not involved with the eye procurement or with the transplant.

*Will the recipient be told who donated the corneas?* The gift of sight is made anonymously. Specific information about the donor family is not available to the recipient. The eye bank will convey a recipient's thanks to the donor family.

*If a person has already signed a donor card or a driver's license, how can they be sure that their wishes regarding donation will be respected?* Tell your family you want to be an eye donor.

*How great is the need for corneas?* Although more than forty-six thousand corneal transplants were performed last year, the need for corneal tissue is never satisfied. While promising advances are being made in artificial corneas, they tend to be reserved for patients with diseases that preclude donor cornea transplantation. Success rates are currently much higher with donor corneas.

*Are there religious objections to eye, organ, or tissue donations?* No. Donation is an opportunity to help save a life or restore someone's sight. Eye, organ, and tissue donation are consistent with the beliefs and attitudes of major religions. For more information on this matter see: Religious Issues. *Brought to you by the* Donor Network of Arizona.

*Is there a fee charged for this donation?* No. It is illegal to buy or sell human eyes, organs, and tissues. Any costs associated with eye procurement are absorbed by the eye bank placing the tissue.

*Is there any delay in funeral arrangements?* No. Eye tissue procurement is performed within hours of death. Families may proceed with funeral arrangements without delay or interruption.

*Will eye donation affect the appearance of the donor?* No. Great care is taken to preserve the donor's appearance. Funeral arrangements, including a viewing if desired, may proceed as scheduled.

*What happens if corneas are not suitable for transplant?* Donors and eyes are carefully evaluated. Corneas determined to be unsuitable for transplant may be used for medical research and teaching.

*How do research and education benefit from eye donation?* Research on glaucoma, retinal disease, eye complications of diabetes, and other sight disorders helps to advance the discovery of the cause and effects of these conditions. This then leads to new treatments and cures.

*What is an eye bank?* An eye bank obtains, medically evaluates, and distributes eyes donated by caring individuals for use in corneal transplantation, research, and education. Eye banks are non-profit organizations.

*How does the eye bank ensure safe corneal tissue for transplantation?* The donated eyes and the donor's medical history are evaluated by the eye bank in accordance with the Eye Bank Association of America's (EBAA) strict Medical Standards. EBAA provides standards for eye banks to use in training personnel to evaluate donor eyes. [19]

# Endnotes

1   *About.com*, "Peter Sinclair," http://quotations.
    about.com/cs/inspirationquotes/a/
    OvercomingAd1/ (accessed August 15, 2008).

2   *About.com*, "William Barclay," http://quotations.
    about.com/cs/inspirationquotes/a/Life5/ (accessed
    August 15, 2008).

3   "Keratoconus definition and images of eye cross-
    sections showing normal and keratoconus
    corneas," © Discovery Eye Foundation,
    http://www.discoveryeyefoundation.org/
    (accessed November 21, 2007).

4   "Cornea Transplant Series," a.d.a.m., Inc.,
    American Accreditation HealthCare Commission,
    http://www.medhelp.org/adam_pages/show_
    section/34234/ (accessed November 21, 2007).

5    *About.com,* "Henry David Thoreau," http://quotations.about.com/od/stillmorefamous people/a/HenryDavidThorı/ (accessed August 15, 2008).

6    *About.com,* "John Wooden," http://quotations. about.com/cs/inspirationquotes/a/Vision6/ (accessed August 15, 2008).

7    "Street Sign Images," Ian McCain © 2006, http://drspinello.com/kcvision/album/ Doublevision/index.html/ (accessed November 21, 2007).

8    *About.com,* "Brian Tracy," http://quotations.about. com/cs/inspirationquotes/a/Confidence6/ (accessed August 15, 2008).

9    *About.com,* "Ralph Waldo Emerson," http://quotations.about.com/cs/inspirationquotes/ a/ Determinationıo/ (accessed August 15, 2008).

10   *Gaia.com,* "Italo Svevo," http://www.gaia.com/ quotes/Italo_Svevo/_(accessed June 18, 2008).

11   *About.com,* "Plato," http://ancienthistory.about. com/library/bl/bl_text_plato_charmides/ (accessed May 21, 2008).

12   *Blueletterbible.org,* "Psalm 119:18," King James Version (KJV), http://www.blueletterbible.org/kjv/ Psa/Psaıı9.html#18, (accessed September 16, 2008).

13     *Cyberhymnal.org*, "Clara H. Fiske Scott,"
http://www.cyberhymnal.org/htm/o/p/openeyes/
(accessed September 16, 2008).

14     *Angel Voices*, "Karen Goldman," http://www.alway
sangels.com/acb-angels/webpage.cfm/
(accessed September 165, 2008).

15     *Quotationsbook.com*, "Richard Halverson," http://
quotationsbook.com/quote/21601/
(accessed September 8, 2008).

16     *About.com*, "Oscar Wilde," http://quotations.about.
com/cs/inspirationquotes/a/Seeing3/
(accessed November 21, 2007).

17     Bob Marley, "I Can See Clearly," Lyrics007.com,
http://www.lyrics007.com/cgi-bin/
s.cgi?q=bob+marley/ (accessed August 12, 2008).

18     *Quotegarden.com*, "Author Unknown,"
http://www.quotegarden.com/blood-organ-
donation/ (accessed September 18, 2008).

19     *Restoresight.org*, "Frequently Asked Questions,"
http://restoresight.org/general/faqs/
(accessed July 25, 2008).